# CEMETERIES
## OF THE STARS

## A JOURNEY TO THE FINAL RESTING PLACES
## OF MUSIC AND FILM LEGENDS

BY RENAE JOHNSON, AUTHOR OF PRECIOUS MEMORIES MEMORIAL

# Special Thanks

To my husband Phil, who has been by my side during this interesting journey
to find the cemeteries of the Stars. You kept me from giving up when the
search was difficult and you took the most incredible photos for my book.
Thank You !!!

ISBN: 978-0-692-10101-8

Renae the Waitress
PO Box 210796
Nashville, TN 37221

NasvhilleMemorialTours.com
Renaethewaitress.com
PreciousMemoriesMemorial.com.

Other Books By Renae Johnson
Precious Memories Memorial
Diary of a TV Waitress
Precious Memories LEGACY

Visit NashvilleMemorialTours.com to take a tour
of the final resting places of the Country Music Legends.

# Table of Contents

# *Introduction*

**The True Tragedy Would Be If They Were Forgotten.**

Taking this journey to locate and visit the final resting places of so many entertainers was a real thrill. Some people feel it's a little odd or it is disrespectful visiting the graves of a movie star or country music singer. Nothing could be further from the truth. These entertainers have spent their entire lives in pursuit of fame. The true tragedy would be if they were forgotten. Visiting these final resting places brought back so many special memories in my life. A song that I heard for the first time while driving in my car, and an old television show that I remember watching with dad before he died. It really was like finding an old friend and sharing memories. These entertainers had made me laugh and cry and I wanted to honor their memory. Standing at their resting places and reading their epitaphs was something I began to look forward to. Here are a few of my favorites:

*"I Will Not Be Right Back After This Message"* – Merv Griffin

*"I Told You I Was Sick"* – Jean Shepard

*"That's All Folks"* – Mel Blanc

*"Together Again"* – George Burns & Gracie Allen

*"If anyone at my funeral has a long face, I'll never speak to them again.'* – Stan Laurel

One of the very special gravesites I visited was that of entertainer Oliver Hardy. As I stood there with tears in my eyes I remembered when our son, Justin, was about 6 years old. He had been attending our church school, The Lord's Chapel, in Brentwood, Tennessee. This one particular day apparently they had a bible lesson from the Old Testament about Lot and his sons. It seemed to bother Justin that Lot's sons received a curse from God for looking upon their father nakedness. As luck would have it…. his Papa Neil was visiting from

Arizona and anxious to pick him up from school. As soon as Justin hopped into the truck and gave his Papa a hug the conversation started! "Papa why do you think God cursed Lot's sons? I take a shower sometimes with my dad?" His Papa was a little stunned and very slow to answer. He knew how smart Justin was and for a split second he wondered if it was a trick question. His papa knew the Bible but he wasn't quite sure how to explain this story to a 6 year old. He finally answered, "Well Justin, when you get to heaven you can ask God that question." Justin immediately answered, "No when I get to heaven I'm going to ask God why Oliver does that thing with his tie. Is it a nervous habit or does he do it just to make me laugh?

Justin was 27 when he got killed in an automobile accident. I often wonder if he ask God about Oliver. Justin loved to laugh and he loved watching the Laurel and Hardy shows. My visit to Laurel and Hardy's final resting places will always be a very special memory.

– Renae.

# 1923-2011

James Arness died in his sleep on Friday, June 3, 2011 at his home in Brentwood, California. He was 88. Arness left behind a touching letter to his fans with the intention it be posted to his website after his death.

"I had a wonderful life and was blessed with so many loving people and great friends. I wanted to take this time to thank all of you for the many years of being a fan of *Gunsmoke, The Thing, How the West Was Won* and all the other fun projects I was lucky enough to have been allowed to be a part of. I had the privilege of working with so many great actors over the years."

James King Aurness (dropped the "u") was born on May 26, 1923, in Minneapolis, Minnesota. He left home at 18 and drifted for a few years before going to college. He was drafted into the Army in 1942 as a rifleman. During a battle, he was severely wounded in his left leg and hospitalized for a year. He was honorably discharged on January 29, 1945, and decorated with the Bronze Star, the Purple Heart, the European-African-Middle Eastern Campaign Medal with three bronze battle stars, the World War II Victory Medal, and the Combat Infantryman Badge. Unfortunately, he left the hospital with a permanent limp. He continued to have acute pain in his leg. He moved to Hollywood in1946 but it was *Gunsmoke* that made him famous. John Wayne, his friend, declined the role and told Arness; "Go ahead and take it, Jim. You're too big for pictures." At six feet, seven inches tall, Arness was believed to be the tallest actor ever to star in a television series. In Gunsmoke's medium-close shots, the other actors were usually standing on elevated platforms, so their faces could be in the camera frame.

Arness played US Marshall Matt Dillon on the hit western TV series, *Gunsmoke* for 20 years, from 1955-1975. For the first 6-½ years *Gunsmoke* was a half hour show, then it expanded to a full hour. It was a top-10 rated show for thirteen of its twenty seasons, and it is still the longest-running dramatic show in prime time TV history. In total, 635 Gunsmoke episodes were filmed, plus five TV movies in the late 1980s and early 1990s, making it the only prime time TV series that ran in five consecutive decades.

Besides Gunsmoke Arness appeared in 34 films and 12 television shows. He refused most interviews over the years and kept his biggest tragedies out of the media. (His daughter and ex-wife both had drug overdoses two years apart). His brother, Peter Graves starred in the hit TV show "Mission Impossible." He used the stage name "Graves," a maternal family name.

# *Final Resting Place*

Forest Lawn Memorial Park
1712 S Glendale Ave
Glendale, CA 91205

# 1916-1987

Jackie Gleason died on June 25, 1987 of colon cancer at his home in Fort Lauderdale, Florida. He was 71. He had just been released from the Imperial Point Medical Center, where he had been undergoing treatment for cancer. In 1986, Jackie was diagnosed with diabetes and phlebitis, but he knew his condition was more serious.

Herbert John Gleason was born February 26, 1916, in Brooklyn, New York. He attended public school and found that humor brightened everything around him. He observed people and created laughter from people's traits. He used his comedy routines in plays and church gatherings. Out of high school he worked as an emcee in carnivals, and then some comedy work. He traveled between New York and Hollywood while working on Broadway in 1940. His first TV show was the "Life of Riley" in 1949.

"The Jackie Gleason Show,'" aired in 1954 with such high ratings that he was given the title of "Mr. Saturday Night." In 1955, Gleason's format changed to accommodate the wild popularity of "The Honeymooners" both owned by Jackie Gleason.

During the 50s and 60s, Gleason recorded 43 albums of mood music, wrote the theme songs "Melancholy Serenade" and "You're My Greatest Love" for his shows.

His huge appetite for food (he could eat five lobsters at a sitting) sometimes pushed his weight up toward 300 pounds. For many years, Gleason was more or less spectacularly obese, and he used to say cheerfully that as a comedian he could ''get away with more as a fat man.'

He won Broadway's 1960 Tony Award as Best Actor (Musical) for *Take Me Along.*

Gleason had parts in over 15 films including the NBC show called "The Honeymooners' Christmas," playing his bus-driver role opposite the durable Mr. Carney. He played a Texas sheriff in "Smokey and the Bandit," an immensely popular action film in 1977.

On August 2000, cable television station TV Land unveiled an eight-foot bronze statue of Gleason as Ralph Kramden. The statue was placed in the Port Authority Bus Terminal in New York City.

## *Celebration of Life*

The closed casket of Jackie Gleason was on view to the public Thursday, June 26 at Lithgow Funeral Home in North Miami.

Gleason's private family memorial mass was held on Saturday, June 28, 1987 at St. Mary's Cathedral in Miami. It was led by Bishop Norbert Dorsey of Miami. During the mass he said, "Throughout his professional life (Jackie) kept the heart of a child. A whimsicalness cheered up a sad and tired world." With his family was actress Audrey Meadows, who played his wife, Alice, in "The Honeymooners" holding a red carnation – a Gleason trademark. Of the mourners who attended, Philip Cuoco, a

*Honeymooners* associate producer commented, "It was a very touching service, very moving. We've lost a pal. Like everybody said, he was the world's greatest."

The church doors swung open nearly an hour after the start of the service to the deep toll of the cathedral's bell. Gleason's bronze casket draped with red carnations was carried to an awaiting brass cart.

## Final Resting Place

Our Lady of Mary Cemetery
11411 NW 25th Street
Miami, FL 33172

"And Away We Go."

## Bette Davis

## 1908-1989

Bette Davis died on Friday night October 6, 1989, at the American Hospital in Paris, France of breast cancer at 81. She had been at the San Sebastian Film Festival in Spain, where she had been honored for her acting. On her return flight to Los Angeles through Paris, France she was admitted to the hospital. Davis had undergone a mastectomy in 1983. She was later told her cancer had spread, and it was terminal, but was encouraged to continue about her business.

Ruth Elizabeth Davis was born April 5, 1908, in Lowell, MA. Her father left when he was seven leaving her and her sister with the feeling of abandonment. She was attending a boarding school in Massachusetts before moving to New York. Davis changed her name to Bette and began pursuing acting. A stock theater company in Rochester, New York hired her for a short stint in a play. In 1929 she made her Broadway debut in *Broken Dishes*. In 1930 she moved to Hollywood and tried to get in movies. She was not successful and was ready to move back to New York when she got a call for the female role in *The Man*

*Who Played God.* She was signed to a 5-year contract with Warner Bros. and stayed with them for the next 18 years. Davis became one of the biggest stars in Hollywood and appeared in around 100 films. Her most notable performances were in the drama *All About Eve* and the hit Agatha Christie mystery *Death on the Nile.* She also appeared on television, winning an Emmy Award for 1979's *Strangers: The Story of Mother and Daughter.* Other awards during her career were from the American Film Institute Life Achievement Award in 1977 and the Kennedy Center Honors Award in 1987.

Bette Davis was married four times. She had a daughter by her third husband and adopted 2 children with her fourth husband, which ended in divorce.

## Celebration of Life

Bette Davis' funeral was delayed due to her body being released and shipped from France. On Thursday morning, October 12, 1989, Bette Davis was laid to rest at Forest Lawn Memorial Park in Burbank, California. The private ceremony and graveside service were restricted to 25 relatives and close friends. Reverend Robert Bock of the First Christian Church in North Hollywood conducted the services.

Thursday, November 2, a memorial service was held at Warner Bros. Stage 18. The list of over 300 actors, writers and directors included Robert Wagner, Roddy McDowell, Angela Lansbury, Stephanie Powers, and Kim Carnes, whose most famous record was 'Bette Davis Eyes.' Actor James Woods gave an emotional tribute to his long-time friend, whom he called '5-feet, 2-inches of dynamite." "Somewhere in heaven there's someone saying 'buckle your seat belt, it's going to be a bumpy eternity."

President Bush sent a telegram saying, "Although she was a self-described terror, all America loved her, and we loved her."

# *Final Resting Place*

Forest Lawn Hollywood Hills
6300 Forest Lawn Drive
Los Angeles, CA 90068

## Oliver "Oliie" Hardy

# 1892-1957

Oliver Hardy died on August 7, 1957 of complications from multiple strokes, with his wife at his side. His last stroke sent him into a coma, from which he never recovered. He was 65. Hardy had suffered a stroke eleven months prior that left him almost completely paralyzed. He was unable to speak and could only use one arm. Stan Laurel would often visit, using hand motions and facial expressions to communicate and amuse one another. During his illness, Oliver wasted away losing his fame bulge of 350 pounds and for some, unrecognizable.

Norvell Hardy was born January 18, 1892 in Harlem, Georgia. He was a gifted singer and, by the age of eight was performing with minstrel shows. He added the first name "Oliver" as a tribute to his father who had died when he was less than a year old, although his friends called him "Babe." During summer vacations he traveled and preformed with Vaudeville acts. While at the University of Georgia studying law he ran a movie theatre and became obsessed with the movie industry. In 1917 he moved to Los Angeles where he began working in films as a comedy actor. Ollie had worked in over 40 films before joining Roach Studios. After signing with Roach he appeared in the 1925 *Wizard Of Oz* as the Tin Man. In 1927, Laurel and Hardy began appearing on the same productions. There was so much positive audience reaction and chemistry they started the *Laurel and Hardy* series. In 1932 they won an Academy Award and in 1947 they went on a six-week tour gaining international success. The two men had a genuine affection for each other, emphasized by Hardy's insistence upon introducing Stan as "my friend, Mr. Laurel."

## Celebration of Life

A Masonic service was held at 1 p.m. at Westwood Valhalla Memorial Park. Family and friends attending included Dick Van Dyke, Alan Mowbray, Hal Roach Jr. and Hal Roach Sr.

Stan Laurel was in poor health and wasn't able to attend his best friend and film partner's funeral, saying, "Babe would understand."

## Final Resting Place

Valhalla Memorial Park
10621 Victory Blvd
North Hollywood, CA 91606

# 1932-1995

Charlie Rich died in his sleep Tuesday, July 25, 1995, in a motel in Hammond, Louisiana on a trip with his wife. The cause of death was a blood clot in his lungs. He was a heavy smoker and had developed a respiratory infection. He was 62.

Charles Allan Rich was born December 14, 1932 in Colt, Arkansas. His parents influenced his musical talent. However it was a black sharecropper on the family land that taught him how to play true "blues" piano. Although he attended college on a football scholarship he transferred to music after an injury. He joined the United States Air Force in 1953 and returned to Memphis playing jazz in clubs and writing music.

In 1958 he became a session musician for Sun Records. In the 60's recorded his own singles but it wasn't until the late 60s working with Bill Sherrill at Epic Records that his smooth sound made him famous. He had a string of hits in the 70s and nine No 1 country singles, including "There Won't Be Anymore," "A Very Special Love Song," "I Don't See Me in Your Eyes Anymore" and "Behind Closed Doors," which sold 1 million copies. In 1973 he had a monster hit with "The Most Beautiful Girl." He had some personal and health problems and retreated from the spotlight in the 80s. Rich released a comeback album in 1992 called "Pictures and Painting," it was his last.

The year after he received the "Entertainer of the Year" by the Country Music Association in 1974, he was asked to be the presenter to the 1975 winner. Prior to the presentation, Rich had a little too much to drink. When he opened the envelope and saw it was to be presented to John Denver, he took a cigarette lighter form his pocket and burned the envelope saying, "The winner is...my friend, John Denver." This was his way of protesting pop music infiltrating into country music. Because of his actions he was banned from future CMA events.

In 1981 Rich retreated to restore his health and personal life. His comeback album, "Pictures and Paintings" was released in 1992 and was well received, but he died shortly after.

## Final Resting Place

Memorial Park Cemetery
5668 Poplar Ave
Memphis, TN 38119

## Vern Gosdin

# 1934-2009

Vern Gosdin died late Tuesday evening April 28, 2009 at a Nashville hospital after suffering a stroke early in April. He was 74. Gosdin had a previous stroke in 1998 but continued to write and sing despite his battle and recovery.

Vernon Gosdin was born April 28, 1934 in Woodland, Alabama, one of nine children who grew up on a farm. He learned to play the guitar and sang on the *Gosdin Family* gospel radio show in Birmingham, Al.

Vern moved to California with his brother in 1961 and became part of the West Coast Country music scene, playing with a few bands as well as teaming up with his brother as a duo act. However, he decided to retire from performing and return back to Alabama to run a glass company. But, as fate would have it, he ended up back in country music with a signed record deal in 1976. He had several hits in the 1970s and '80s including "Set 'em Up Joe," "I Can Tell by the Way You Dance," and "I'm Still Crazy."

In 1989 "Chiseled in Stone" was voted *Song of the Year* by the Country Music Association. In the song, an older man tells a younger man who is going through tough times, "You don't know about sadness 'til you faced life alone, you don't know about lonely 'til it's chiseled in stone." He used life experiences in his music. Gosdin, also known as "The Voice," had 19 top 10 solo hits on the country music charts from 1977 through 1990. In 2005, he was inducted into the Alabama Music Hall of Fame.

During his career, he sang gospel music, bluegrass, folk-rock and country. He had a rich baritone, and was once described by Tammy Wynette as "the only other singer who can hold a candle to George Jones." (That was a huge compliment since George was his idol.)

## Celebration of Life

There was a public visitation on Saturday at Mount Olivet Funeral Home from 12-4 p.m. A private service followed.

## Final Resting Place

Mt. Olivet Cemetery
1101 Lebanon Pike
Nashville, TN 37210

Burt Lancaster

1913-1994

**B**urt Lancaster died overnight Thursday, October 22, 1994 of a heart attack at his home. His health had been failing after a stroke four years earlier while visiting a friend. He refused visitors as his health worsen, even his old friend, Kirk Douglas. He was 80.

Burton Stephen Lancaster was born November 2, 1913, in New York. He was 6 feet, 2 inches tall by the time he was 14. With his big physique and quick reflexes he got an athletic scholarship to New York University. However he quit college to join the Kay Brothers Circus as an acrobat until an injury in 1939. In 1942 he joined the Army and performed with the Army's 21st Special Services Division. After serving his country, Lancaster auditioned for a Broadway play staring as an Army sergeant. In 1946, Lancaster made his movie debut opposite Ava Gardner in *The Killers. From Here to Eternity* earned him his first Oscar nomination.

In 1983 Lancaster underwent multiple coronary artery bypass surgery, and continued to suffer from a heart condition. Lancaster bounced back for a heralded performance in *Field of Dreams* in 1989.

Lancaster was in 70 films and was nominated four times for Academy Awards. The American Film Institute ranked him as #19 greatest male star.

## Celebration of Life

Lancaster requested no funeral or memorial service be held.

## Final Resting Place

Westwood Memorial Park
1218 Glendon Ave
Los Angeles, CA 90024

# 1909-1994

THE ADVENTURES OF
Ozzie
and
Harriet

Harriet Nelson died Sunday afternoon, October 2, 1994 at her Laguna Beach, California home holding her son, David's hand. She died of congestive heart failure at 85. It was reported, "she fell asleep and passed away peacefully."

Harriet had been hospitalized for three weeks and was released on Friday at her request. She was a heavy smoker and had a long battle with emphysema. She had remained out of public view since her husband's death in 1975 and her son's death in 1986.

Peggy Lou Snyder was born July 18, 1909 in Des Moines, Iowa. She first appeared in vaudeville at age three and went on to perform on Broadway, later becoming a singer in Ozzie's band.

"The Adventures of Ozzie and Harriet," which began on radio in 1944 and aired on television from 1952 to 1966, was the longest-running family sitcom in TV history. In the process of producing 435 episodes, the Nelsons became an American institution. Long after the show was canceled, people would still approach Harriet and say, "Aren't you Ozzie and Harriet?" She'd always laugh and say, "Well, I'm one of them."

# *Celebration of Life*

A private memorial service was held on Thursday, October 6, 1994 at Church of the Hills. The service was played on a public address system outside the church for reporters. As the 150-200 friends and family arrived, they heard the recordings of Ozzie Nelson's dance band music from the 1930s. During the 1 ½ hour service her twin grandsons performed "Love Me Today—Tomorrow I'll Be Gone" a song written after the death of her son, Rick. David Nelson shared that his mom had told him, "Whatever you do don't have a memorial service "for me." Drawing a lot of laughter when he said, "So I'm in a lot of trouble." He said he was certain his parents and brother have been reunited in heaven. Other speakers included granddaughter, actress Tracy Nelson.

# *Final Resting Place*

Forest Lawn Hollywood Hills
6300 Forest Lawn Dr
Los Angeles, CA 90068

Harriet was cremated and her remains were interred on a hillside next to her husband, Ozzie and son, Rick.

HARRIET H. NELSON
BELOVED WIFE AND MOTHER
1909 - 1994

## Troy Gentry

## 1967-2017

Troy Gentry was killed in a helicopter accident on September 8, 2017 in Medford, New Jersey. He was 50. Cause of the crash was a result of engine failure. Gentry and his duet partner, Eddie Montgomery were scheduled to perform that evening at the Flying W Airport & Resort. According to a preliminary incident report by the NTSB, "Several minutes after takeoff, the pilot reported that he was unable to control engine RPM with throttle inputs." The helicopter landed short of the runway in low brush. The helicopter ride was described as an impromptu, spur of the moment, unplanned moment decision. It was a "Would you like to go for a helicopter ride?" The day started with Montgomery Gentry arriving with folks anxious and excited to hear the best concert ever. It never happened.

Troy Lee Gentry was born April 5, 1967 in Lexington, Kentucky. He was best known as a member of the famous country duo, Montgomery Gentry.

They began in 1999 with their debut album, *Tattoos & Scars*. Their sound was known as Southern rock and country and they had a string of No.1 hits, including "If You Ever Stop Loving Me," "Something to Be Proud Of," "Lucky Man," "Back When I Knew It All" and "Roll With Me" receiving platinum and gold status. Gentry was honored with the Academy of Country Music's Humanitarian Award in 2009.

## Celebration of Life

Gentry's 80-mintue memorial service was held at 11 a.m., Thursday, September 14, 2017 at the Grand Ole Opry House. Radio personality Storme Warren hosted the service with 1500 family, friends and fans gathered to mourn Gentry. Little Big Town began the service with "The Star-Spangled Banner." Other artists who performed were Halfway 2 Hazard, who performed "My Old Kentucky Home," Trace Adkins sang "Wayfaring Stranger" and Charlie Daniels, "How Great Thou Art." Vince Gill brought everyone to tears with "Whenever You Come Around." The service concluded with a song Gentry recently recorded called "Better Me."

Among the celebrities in attendance were his musical partner, Eddie Montgomery, Keith Urban, Travis Tritt, Randy Owen, and Randy Travis, to name a few.

In lieu of flowers, Gentry's family ask that donations be made to T.J. Martell Foundation or The American Red Cross for hurricane relief.

## Final Resting Place

Unknown

## Mel Tillis

## 1932-2017

Mel Tillis died on November 19, 2017 in Munroe Regional Medical Center in Ocala, Florida. Although he had a lengthy battle with intestinal issues, the cause of death was suspected respiratory failure. He had surgery in 2016 and spent weeks in intensive care fighting sepsis.

Lonnie Melvin Tillis was born on August 8, 1932, in Tampa Florida. Tillis had malaria as a child, leaving him with a speech impediment. He embraced his stuttering as an adult and used it for a comic effect in his performances. It soon became his trademark. As a boy he taught himself to play guitar, playing a parties and events. He attended the University of Florida and joined the U.S. Air Force and formed a country band that aired on Armed Forces Radio. After the service in 1957 he moved to Nashville to pursue a music career and song writing.

His first break came when Webb Pierce recorded his song, "I'm Tired." He was able to secure a recording deal in 1958. Other recording successes were "Good Woman Blues," "Wine," and "Coca-Cola Cowboy" which was featured in the Clint Eastwood film *Every Which Way But Loose* and of course "Detroit City."

In addition to his music he had some minor movie roles in *Smokey and the Bandit II* and *The Cannonball Run*. He also appeared on television shows like *Hee Haw* and *Hollywood Squares*.

Tillis recorded over 60 albums, with 36 Top Ten singles. He wrote over 1,000 songs including some classics.

In the 1990's Tillis, Waylon Jennings, Bobby Bare and Jerry Reed formed a super group called "Old Dogs" and released an album.

Tillis was inducted into the Nashville Songwriters Hall of Fame in 1976 and he was inducted into the Country Music Hall of Fame in 2007.

## Celebration of Life

### November 25 - Florida

Family and Friends celebrated the life of Mel Tillis at Ocklawaha Bridge Baptist Church, Saturday, November 19th. His brown casket was covered with the American flag. Pastor Jared Buchanan led the service. Tommy Tillis, Tillis' cousin sang a song in memory of Tillis. Pam Tillis thanked the nurses at MRMC and her father's caretakers. She also asked that those gathered at the church remember her father for such things as loving the Florida Gators, the sport of fishing, and his appearances at the Florida Strawberry Festival, the author Mark Twain and other things that her father held dear.

### November 27 - Tennessee

Mel Tillis public funeral was at 3 p,m. on Monday, November 27, 2017 in Clarksville Tennessee at Mt. Hermon Baptist Church. His casket was covered with a spray of red roses with floral arrangements that surrounded his photo. Steve Murphee, Mel's long time pastor spoke. His daughter, country singer Pam Tillis gave the eulogy. Daughter, Carrie Tillis sang, "His Eye is on the Sparrow". Bobby Tomberlin and two of Mel Tillis' "Stutterettes" backup singers sang gospel music during the ceremony.

Among the stars attending were Charley Pride, Jeannie Seely, Bobbie Bare, Teea Goans, and more.

# *Final Resting Place*

Tillis was laid to rest during a private burial in the Tillis family plot.

Woodall Cemetery
Hwy 12 (behind Mt. Herman Baptist Church)
Clarksville, TN 37043

## Alan Ladd (Shane)

## 1913-1964

Alan Ladd died January 29, 1964 from an apparent accidental overdose (some believed he committed suicide) of alcohol and sedatives at his home in Palm Springs, California. He was 50. His butler said he saw Ladd seemingly asleep in his bed at 10 a.m. When he returned at 3:30 p.m. he checked on Ladd again and found him still there and dead. Throughout his life, Ladd suffered badly from insomnia and found solace in sedatives and an ever-increasing dependence on alcohol.

Alan Walbridge Ladd was born September 3, 1913 in Hot Springs, Arkansas. His father died when Alan was four years old. When Ladd was five he accidentally burned his home down by playing with matches. His family moved to North Hollywood where he was raised and attended North Hollywood High School. In high school Ladd was a swimmer who won swimming and diving championships. His first appearance in a movie was an aquatic show, *Marinella* in July 1933.

On November 29, 1937 Ladd's mother, who was staying with him following the breakup of a relationship, asked Ladd for some money to buy something at a local store. Ladd gave her the money, thinking it was for alcohol. She purchased some arsenic-based ant paste from a grocer and committed suicide by drinking it in the back seat of Ladd's car.

In 1941 Ladd had instant success when he appeared as a psychopathic killer in a low budget sleeper, *This Gun for Hire*. For over a decade his career continued to strengthen as he starred in many films for Paramount, quickly establishing himself as one of the top leading men in Hollywood. In 1946 he produced and starred in three hit movies: *Two Years Before the Mast*, the spy thriller *O.S.S.*, and another classic film opposite Veronica Lake, *The Blue Dahlia*.

He will always be remembered as the title character in *Shane* in 1953. It's considered to be one of the greatest of all Westerns. He appeared in 47 movies during his career.

Even with a successful career and a squeaky clean image, he referred to himself as "the most insecure guy in Hollywood. In 1962 Ladd was found with a bullet lodged in his chest that was reported as an attempted suicide by shooting himself. He had a full recovery.

Ladd was married twice and had 3 children. Alan Ladd, Jr., is a film executive and producer and founder of the Ladd Company. Actress Alana Ladd, who co-starred with her father in *Guns of the Timberland* and *Duel of Champions*, is married to the veteran talk radio broadcaster Michael Jackson. Actor David Ladd, who co-starred with his father as a child in *The Proud Rebel*, was married to *Charlie's Angels* star Cheryl Ladd.

## Celebration of Life

Ladd's funeral was held on February 1, 1964, with Edmond O'Brien giving the eulogy. Fans were allowed to see his coffin. He was buried with a letter his son, David, had written him.

# Final Resting Place

Forrest Lawn Memorial Park
1712 S. Glendale Ave
Glendale, CA 91025

1913 — 1964

BELOVED HUSBAND AND FATHER

IN THIS HEART OF MINE..
YOU LIVE ALL THE TIME...

## John Ritter

## 1948-2003

John Ritter died Thursday, September 11, 2003 from an undetected flaw in his heart called an aortic dissections, a heart defect which is a weak blood vessel/wall that burst if not detected. He collapsed Thursday while on the set of his ABC comedy *8 Simple Rules For Dating MY Teenage Daughter*. He was taken across the street to Providence St. Joseph Hospital in Burbank, California. He was 54.

Jonathan Southworth Ritter was born in Burbank, California on September 17. 1948. He was the son of legendary country singer/actor Tex Ritter and actress Dorothy Fay. He graduated from the University of Southern California in 1971 with a drama degree.

After playing guest roles on shows like *The Walton's*, he landed the role of Jack Tripper on the hit TV series *Three's Company*, which won him an Emmy. The series aired from 1977-1984. In 1984 Ritter formed his own production company, Adams Productions. He produced and starred in the comedy-drama *Hooperman*.

He starred in more than 25 TV movies and 50 plays and has a Star on the Hollywood Walk of Fame by his father's Tex Ritter.

## Celebration of Life

Family and close friends mourned the passing of John Ritter on Monday, September 15, 2003 at a private funeral service held in Los Angeles.

## Final Resting Place

Forest Lawn Hollywood Hills
6300 Forest Lawn Drive
Los Angeles, CA 90068

Beloved Husband, Father, Brother, Son and Friend.

"And in the end, the love you take is equal to the love you make"
~ The Beatles.

Bud Abbott died on April 24, 1974 in Woodland Hills, California at the age of 76. He was a lifelong epileptic who died of prostate cancer following two strokes.

He was broke, living off a small monthly social security benefit. A man who brought so much laughter to so many people felt forgotten. His wife worked part time, and his children supported him. In the 70s Abbott had a series of stokes, followed by a broken hip, and prostate cancer. In Bud Abbott's final months, he basically faded away in a hospital bed in what was once a dining room. He died surrounded by his family.

William Alexander Abbott was born October 2, 1897 in Ashbury Park, New Jersey as a twin. Both of his parents had worked for the Barnum and Bailey Circus. Abbott worked in carnivals after dropping out of school and later became a straight man performing in vaudeville. In 1931 he substituted for comic Lou Costello's straight man and the two clicked almost immediately. They soon formed their famous comedy team.

In 1940 he made his film debut in *One Night in the Tropics* with partner Lou Costello. He had been in several movies in the 1920's.

Abbott was known as one of the best "straight men" in the entertainment world. Earnings with his partner were 40/60 split.  He believed comics were a dime a dozen.  Good straight men are hard to find.

The performance of "Who's on First?" in the film *The Naughty Nineties* (1945) is one of the most famous memorable stints.

Soon after former partner Lou Costello died in 1959, the Internal Revenue Service demanded Bud pay over $750,000 in back taxes. He was forced to sell his estate in Encino, California (at a loss), as well as his 200-acre ranch. His wife sold her jewelry and furs and they relinquished their remaining share of profits from the old lucrative Universal movies. He said he'd have to start all over and asked for donations from Abbott & Costello fans, with little results.

# Final Resting Place

He was cremated and his ashes were scattered in the Pacific Ocean.

*Abbott and Costello each have three stars on the Hollywood Walk of Fame for their work in radio, television and motion pictures.*

1943-1997

John Denver died Sunday, October 13, 1997 in a plane crash. He was 53. Denver was piloting the two-seat light plane along the California coast when the engine failed shortly after 5 p.m., plunging him into ocean waters just past Monterey Bay. It was reported that Denver was a very experienced pilot and was practicing taking off and landing when the accident occurred.

Denver was in a previous plane accident in April 1989. He walked away uninjured after the 1931 biplane he was piloting spun around while taxiing at an airport in northern Arizona.

Henry John Deutschendorf was born December 31, 1943 in Roswell, New Mexico. He traveled throughout his childhood and adopted his stage name from the Colorado capital. After studying architecture at Texas Tech, he went west in 1965 to pursue a career in folk music. It was the folk group Peter, Paul and Mary that recorded his big hit "Leaving On A Jet Plane" that became a #1 song in the country.  In 1971 Denver charted his own singing hit, "Take Me Home, Country Road" that gained him worldwide fame as a singer.  He had a string of hits that followed including, "Rocky Mountain High," "Thank God I'm a Country Boy" and "Annie's Song."

In 1977, Denver made his big-screen acting debut in *Oh, God,* opposite George Burns. He continued to made occasional acting appearances over the years, but was better known for his television specials. Denver appeared in several Christmas shows, including two with Jim Henson's Muppets.

## Celebration of Life

More than 1000 fans, friends and family members gathered at a memorial service on Friday, October 17, 1997 for John Denver. The 10:00 a.m. service was held at the Faith Presbyterian Church in Aurora, Colorado with Pastor Les Felker officiating.  A good friend, Tom Crumb,  and Denver's brother, Ron Deutschendorf spoke at his memorial.  At the front of the church surrounded by flowers was a large picture of the Denver.

A separate service was held on Saturday, October 18, 1997 in Aspen, Colorado. This service not only included Denver's friends and brother, but Denver's ex-wife, Annie, who spoke.

# Final Resting Place

Denver was cremated and his ashes were scattered in the Rocky Mountains.

On September 23, 2007, nearly ten years after Denver's death, his brother Ron witnessed the dedication of a plaque placed near the crash site in Pacific Grove, California, commemorating the singer.

## Audrey Meadows

## 1926-1996

Audrey Meadows died Saturday at 8:50 p.m. on February 3, 1996 after slipping into a coma. She died at Cedars-Sinai Medical Center in Los Angeles of lung cancer. Her sister was by her side. She was 69.

She was diagnosed with lung cancer and given a year to live. She declined all treatment and concealed the terminal illness from her sister and brother-in-law, entertainers Jayne Meadows and Steve Allen. She did not reveal her illness until she was hospitalized Jan. 24. She had been a chain-smoker.

Audrey Cotter was born February 8, 1926 in WuChang, China and spent her first six years there as the daughter of a missionary. Her family returned back to the US and settled in New England. Audrey and her sister, Jayne Meadows, attended an all-girls boarding school in NY. It was because of Jayne she also changed her name to Meadows. After high school they both stuck together and pursued the entertainment field. Audrey trained as a coloratura soprano and made her singing debut at New York's Carnegie Hall when she was 16 and began performing in Broadway shows. Her first TV roles were all the female roles on NBC's "Bob ad Ray Show."

She joined "The Honeymooners" in 1955 as Alice Kramden. Her bus driver husband, Ralph, threatened her weekly with a trip to the moon on the TV series. Although she was the second actress to play that role, she was the most well known. When she first auditioned for the part of Alice, Gleason turned her down saying she was too pretty and no one would believe her to be Ralph Kramden's wife. She was so determined that she sent photos of herself with no makeup and frumpy clothes. Gleason, not recognizing her, thought she was perfect and hired her. She was in thirty-nine half hour episodes.

Audrey telephoned Gleason shortly before his death in 1987, telling him, "Jackie, it's Audrey, it's your Alice. I just called to tell you I loved you ... . I never thanked you for giving me the part of Alice." He replied, "I knew what I was doing."

## *Celebration of Life*

There was a private service for family members and close friends. In lieu of flowers, the family asked for contributions be made to the American Red Cross.

# *Final Resting Place*

Holy Cross Catholic Cemetery
5835 W. Slauson Ave
Culver City, CA 90230

## Jean Shepard

# 1933-2016

Jean Shepard died Sunday, September 25, 2016 from Parkinson's disease. She was 82.

Ollie Imogene Shepard was born Nov. 21, 1933 in Pauls Valley, Oklahoma and the daughter of a sharecropper. She grew up singing in church and listening to the music of Jimmie Rodgers and Bob Wills. Her family moved to Visalia, California around the age of 11. While in high school she became part of the "Melody Ranch Girls" band and sang on a radio show.

In 1952, Hank Thompson came to her town and heard her sing. A few months later he helped get her a record deal with Capitol Records. There were very few female artists at that time but it was her duet with Ferlin Husky in 1952, "A Dear John Letter," that landed her notoriety. It sold more than a million records and spent six weeks on the country charts; "A Dear John Letter" also hit No. 4 on the pop charts. When Shepard began working with Husky, she was younger than 21. Her parents had to make him her legal guardian so that the two singers could tour together across state lines. Ferlin taught her a lot about the music business in those early years. And it was some of those lessons that helped her survive both success and tragedy.

On her 22 birthday she was ask to join the Grand Ole Opry, making her the third female member. (Kitty Wells and Minnie Pearl were the other two). In 1960 her and Hawkshaw Hawkins toured together and married in November. She had one son, Don Robin, before Hawkins was killed in a plane crash on March 5, 1963. Shortly after the crash, she gave birth to their second son, Harold Franklin.

Shepard continued her successful recording and touring career. She had 73 songs on the country charts. On November 21, 2015, the Grand Ole Opry celebrated Shepard's 60th anniversary as a member.

## Celebration of Life

A public funeral was held on Friday September 30, 2016. Visitation was scheduled from 11–1 p.m at the Hendersonville Funeral Home's chapel with the funeral at 1:00 p.m. Family, friends and fellow Grand Ole Opry members gathered to bid her farewell. Opry announcer Eddie Stubbs gave a moving Eulogy with many in the chapel laughing through their tears remembering the legend sharing memories of her sharp wit, legendary toughness and feisty personality.

At the end of the service she was given her final standing ovation to the lady who captivated and entertained so many. Friends and family filed past her open casket at the end of the service as her 1955 hit "Satisfied Mind" played softly. Opry friends who attended included, Bill Anderson, Jan Howard, Connie Smith, Jimmy Capps, Keith Bilbrey to name a few.

Hendersonville Memory Gardens
353 E. Main Street
Hendersonville, TN 37075

## Brian Keith

## 1921-1997

Brian Keith took his own life on Tuesday, June 24, 1997. Police were called to his Malibu, California home at 10:13 a.m. and found Keith with a gunshot wound to his head. In 1997 he was diagnosed with lung cancer and emphysema, despite having quit smoking ten years earlier. Difficult chemotherapy treatments and grief over his daughter, Daisy who committing suicide in April took an emotional toll on him. It was also reported that he had financial problems and suffered from depression throughout his final days. He was 75.

There was a hand written note left:

*"The end is here. I'm finished. The pain is too much. Now it's time for me to join our little Daisy. She needs me. She didn't want to be without me here, so she'll have me again over there. Don't be sad. This had to come soon."*

Robert Alba Keith was born November 14, 1921 in Bayonne, New Jersey. Both of his parents were in show business but Keith lived with his father after their divorce. He appeared with his father in his first movie, *Pied Piper Malone*, at age three. He continued acting and appeared in radio programs and stage until he joined the Marines. He served in World War II from 1941-1945 as a Radio-Gunner in the US Marines. After the service he began as a stage actor but branched out into film and television.

In 1952 he made his debut on episodes of *Tales of Tomorrow*, then appeared in such shows as *Police Story, The United States Steel Hour, The Pepsi-Cola Playhouse* and *The Adventures of Ellery Queen*. In 1955 he starred in his won series, *Crusaders*. He continued to have guest roles on TV series like *Rawhide, Laramie, The Untouchables, Wagon Train, The Fugitive, The Virginian* and *Zane Grey Theater*. Starring roles in series he gained fame from in the 60s was *Parent Trap, The Westerner, Nevada Smith*.

In 1966, Keith landed the role of Uncle Bill Davis on CBS's popular television situation comedy *Family Affair*. This role earned him three Emmy Award nominations for Best Actor in a Comedy Series. The show made him a household name.

Keith's TV work also included the 1972-74 sitcom, *The Brian Keith Show*, and *Hardcastle & McCormick*.

He was honored with a star on the Hollywood Walk of Fame on June 26, 2008. His widow, Victoria Young Keith, asked that his star be placed near to that of Walt Disney. The committee graciously complied and now these two good friends have stars next to each other.

# *Celebration of Life*

There was a private family funeral. *Family Affair* co-stars Kathy Garver and Johnny Whitaker, and *Hardcastle and McCormick* co-star Daniel Hugh Kelly attended with family members.

# Final Resting Place

Pierce Bros Westwood Village Memorial Park
1218 Glendon Ave
Los Angeles, CA 90024

Keith's ashes were interred above those of his daughter Daisy.

## Jack Webb

## 1920-1982

Webb died on December 23, 1982 at his home in Los Angeles of an apparent heart attack at age 62.

John Randolph Webb was born on April 2, 1920 in Santa Monica, California. He lived in a parish and served as an altar boy before attending Belmont High School in Los Angeles. He studied Art at St. John's University in Minnesota and also served a short time in the US Army before getting a hardship discharge. He moved to San Francisco where he became a radio announcer.

*The Jack Webb Show* was a half-hour comedy and aired until 1946. By 1949, he had given up comedy for drama. His most notable motion picture role was in the *The D.I.* but it wasn't a big success.

Web conceived and created the *Dragnet* concept, based on actual police files. He got the role of Sgt. Joe Friday. *Dragnet* premiered on NBC Radio in 1949 and ran till 1957. It was also picked up as a television series by NBC, which aired from 1952 to 1959. Due to it's popularity Webb brought it back to television in 1967 for four more seasons. He was the star, the director, the producer and the executive producer.

In *Dragnet's* early days, Webb continued to appear in movies, notably as the best friend of William Holden's character in the 1950 Billy Wilder film *Sunset Boulevard*. In 1950, Webb appeared alongside future 1960s *Dragnet* partner Harry Morgan in the film noir *Dark City*.

Web started a production company and produced or co-produced the following TV series: *Dragnet, Adam-12, Emergency, US Treasury, Project U.F.O.* and *Sierra*.

He has two stars on the Hollywood Walk of Fame. One for Radio and one for Television and he was also inducted into the Television Hall of Fame.

## Celebration of Life

Webb was given a funeral with full police honors. On Webb's death, it was announced that badge No. 714, which was used by Joe Friday in Dragnet, would be retired. Los Angeles Mayor Tom Bradley ordered all flags lowered to half-staff in Webb's honor for a day. Webb was buried with a replica LAPD badge bearing the rank of sergeant and the No. 714.

*The story you have just seen is true.*
*The names were changed to protect the innocent.*

# Final Resting Place

Forest Lawn Hollywood Hills
6300 Forest Lawn Drive
Los Angeles, CA 90068

*"Just the Facts, Ma'am"*

## Hank Thompson

# 1925-2007

Hank Thompson died at 10:45 p.m. on Tuesday night, November 7, 2007, at his home in Fort Worth, Texas. He had been battling aggressive lung cancer and canceled his tour just days before. He passed away peacefully with friends and family at his side. He was 82.

Henry William Thompson was born on September 3, 1925 in Waco, Texas. He grew up as a fan of Gene Autry, which inspired him to learn how to play the guitar. He first performed as a teenager on a local station as *Hank the Hired Hand*, singing the songs of childhood and current country favorites.

Thompson enlisted in the U.S. Navy right out of high school and continued his interest in writing and entertaining. After his discharge in 1946 he attended college at Southern Methodist University in Dallas and eventually wound up back in Waco on radio station KWTX, who gave him a prime time spot. He started performing locally and put together a band called the *Brazos Valley Boys*.

His first recording was "Whoa, Sailor" in 1946, after getting the attention of Tex Ritter who helped him get his record contract. Hank had a very distinctive voice that fans loved and a mix of honky-tonk and western swing style. While Thompson enjoyed a respectable string of hits in the late 1940s, which included "Humpty Dumpty Heart," "Swing Wide Your Gate Of Love," "Six Pack To Go," and the Jack and Woody Guthrie song "Oklahoma Hills." It was his 1952 recording of "The Wild Side Of Life" that really boosted his career. He had 29 hits reach the top ten between 1948-1975.

Becoming one of the most popular dance bands in the country Thompson and his band dressed for "showbiz." They wore colorful Western outfits made by Nude Cohen, a tailor outside Los Angeles. His band, the *Brazos Valley Boys,* received many awards during Hank's career. They made Billboard magazine's touring band of the year award 14 consecutive times.

Thompson cut several groundbreaking concept albums in the 1950s, and he pioneered the live country music concert album with "Live at the Golden Nugget" from Las Vegas (1961), then followed this up with other "on location" albums — from the *Cheyenne Frontier Days Rodeo* (July 1962) and back in his home state at the State Fair of Texas (October 1962), where Thompson and his *Brazos Valley Boys* were regularly featured each fall for years. In the 60s Thompson, a Commercial and Airline Transport Pilot, purchased a twin engine 6 passenger Cessna 310 and flew to many of his shows.

He performed on seven continents, and continued to record and tour into the 21st century, earning him the distinction of a seven-decade career. He was inducted into the Country Music Hall of Fame in 1989 and inducted into the Songwriters Hall of Fame in 1997.

## Celebration of Life

Thompson requested that no funeral be held. However a "celebration," was held for fans and friends, on November 14th. The location was fitting for Thompson: "Billy Bob's Texas," a Fort Worth Texas honky-tonk.

# Final Resting Place

Waco Memorial Park
6623 S. Interstate 35
Waco, TX 76702

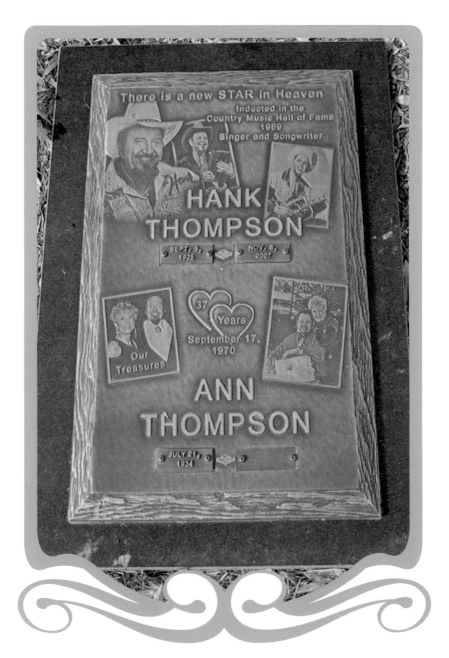

## Dean Martin

## 1917-1995

D ean Martin died on December 25, 1995 at his home in Beverly Hills, California of lung cancer. He was 78. Martin, a heavy smoker, was diagnosed with lung cancer at Cedars Sinai Medical Center in September 1993, and was told that he would require surgery to prolong his life, but he rejected it.

Dino Paul Crocetti was born June 7, 1917 in Steubenville, Ohio. He began his singing career in a local spaghetti parlor. As a teenager he was an amateur fighter. He adopted the name Dean Martin after meeting Jerry Lewis. In 1946, the singer happened to be booked on the same bill at the 500 Club in Atlantic City. Dean said, "We would horse around and do anything that came to our minds." Their chemistry became apparent and spread quickly. They were soon offered a long-term movie deal. *My Friend Irma,* made in 1949, was the first of 16 films they made together. In 1956 after finishing their final picture they announced their breakup. Martin became a television star in 1965 when *The Dean Martin Show,* began its eight-year run.

He appeared in 55 films while his recording career was just as successful. He had 40 singles on Billboard's chart between 1950 and 1969. "That's Amore" (1953), "Memories Are Made of This" (1955), and "Everybody Loves Somebody" (1964) – were million-sellers.

As Martin's solo career grew, he and Frank Sinatra became friends. In the late 1950s and early 1960s, Martin and Sinatra, along with friends Joey Bishop, Peter Lawford, and Sammy Davis, Jr. formed the Rat Pack. The Rat Pack was legendary for its Las Vegas Strip performances.

## Celebration of Life

When Martin died the lights of the Las Vegas Strip were dimmed in his honor. An invitation only private memorial service was held at 7 p.m. Thursday, December 28th at Pierce Brothers Westwood Village Memorial Park. There were to be no sermons, no sad stories-only happy remembrances. There was no casket in the chapel, instead a beautiful picture of Dean at the microphone, a flag of Italy and flowers alongside.

Those in attendance were Martin's longtime friends Jerry Lewis, Don Rickles, Bob Newhart, Shirley Mac-Laine, Robert Stack, Nancy Sinatra, Tony Danza, Angie Dickinson, Tony Martin and Dorothy Hamill, Janet Leigh, Tony Curtis and Dom DeLuise and more.

Rosemary Clooney started the evening singing "Everybody Loves Somebody Sometime." The first person to speak was Shirley MacLaine. She said, "Well, the last time I spoke to Dean ... was about an hour ago and he said everything is fine." Everyone broke into laughter (knowing her strong belief in the afterlife). She then talked about her love for Dean and their more than 40-year friendship.

Lewis read his emotional tribute: "We're here to celebrate his 78 years." He spoke of Dean's "exquisite tranquility despite a great inner turbulence." He said Dean "had steel balls." He closed by saying to Dean, "Rest well and don't forget to short-sheet my bed when I get there." Jerry was in tears after his remarks and those of the others.

For a final toast, they were treated to Dean's favorite songs, sung by him, on a special CD. The songs included: "You're Nobody Till Somebody Loves You," "Memories Are Made of This," "That's Amore," "Little Old Winemaker, Me," "Houston," "The Glory of Love," "Red Roses For a Blue Lady," "Make the World Go Away" and "Volare."

In lieu of flowers, mourners had been asked to make donations to a charity - Barbara Sinatra's Children's Center at the Eisenhower Medical Center in Rancho Mirage, Calif.

## Final Resting Place

Westwood Memorial Park
1218 Glendon Ave
Los Angeles, CA 90024

"Everybody Loves Somebody Sometime" is written on his crypt.

DEAN MARTIN
JUNE 7, 1917 - DECEMBER 25, 1995
EVERYBODY LOVES SOMEBODY SOMETIME

## Dan Seals

## 1948-2009

Dan Seals died Wednesday night March 25, 2009 at his daughter's home in Nashville, Tennessee of complications from cancer. He was 61. Seals was diagnosed with lymphoma two years earlier and had participated in several clinical trials to assist with research on his type of lymphoma.

Dan Seals was born February 8, 1948 in McCamey, Texas. His father, an accomplished musician, played with such Texas singers as Bob Wills, Ernest Tubb, and Jim Reeves and taught Dan to play upright bass and guitar. It was after moving to Dallas and attending high school that he formed a band with his classmate, John Coley, and began playing with artists coming into town. In 1960 the duo moved to Los Angeles and began performing as *England Dan and John Ford Coley*. Seals used the name England Dan because he loved the Beatles and even used an English accent as they pursued a different sound. It was several years before they recorded and released the smash hit "I'd Really Love To See You Tonight" selling more than two million copies. Other top hits included "Nights are Forever Without You," We'll Never Have to Say Goodbye Again" and "Love Is the Answer."

The duo split in the 80s and Seals moved to Nashville to pursue a solo career. He then decided to record as Dan Seals. His country hits in the '80s and '90s included "Bop," "You Still Move Me," "Love on Arrival," and a duet with Marie Osmond, "Meet Me in Montana."

Seals started spending more time with his family and his Baha'i faith as the country music industry started changing in the 90s. He still continued to perform with his brother as a duo, Seals & Seals until he got sick. They were working on a new album but never finished it.

## Celebration of Life

A pubic memorial service was held March 28 at 1 p.m. at the Baha'i Faith Church 1556 Bell Road Nashville, TN 37211

The family requested that flowers not be sent.

## Final Resting Place

Public burial was a 3:30 p.m.
Woodlawn Memorial Park
660 Thompson Lane
Nashville, TN 37204

## Red Skelton

# 1913-1997

R ed Skelton died on September 17, 1997 at the Eisenhower Medical Center in Rancho Mirage, California from pneumonia at the age of 84.

Richard Bennett Skelton was born July 18, 1913 in Vincennes, Indiana. At age seven he was singing on the streets for money. When he was 10 he joined the Medicine Show and continued playing minstrel shows on riverboats. In 1937, he debuted on Broadway and also was on radio. It was Mickey Rooney in 1938 who arranged for MGM studios to sign him for his first movie, *Having a Wonderful Time* starring Douglas Fairbanks and Ginger Rogers.

He appeared in 43 movies starting back in the 40s and 50s and in such comedy greats as *Panama Hattie*, *A Southern Yankee*, *Whistling in Dixie* and *Whistling in Brooklyn*.

He had a repertoire of characters that included:

Clem Kadiddlehopper - a slow-witted country bumpkin

Cauliflower McPugg - the punch-drunk prizefighter

Sheriff Deadeye - the lawman of the old west

San Fernando Red - the con man Bolivar Shagnasty

Gertrude and Heathcliff - the cross-eyed sea gulls

Mean Widdle Kid - who created "I dood it."

Freddie the Freeloader - a hobo that never spoke

Willie Lump-Lump - the drunk

Although famous for his "drunk" comedy sketches, he never drank and was, in fact, allergic to alcohol.

In 1944 Skelton was inducted into the Army as a private, assigned first to field artillery then to an entertainment unit. He suffered what was described as a nervous breakdown but remained in the Army, entertaining troops in the United States until his discharge in 1945.

*The Red Skelton Show* started as a radio show in the 1940. By 1951 it became a television shows and remained on television ending a successful 30-year career in 1971.

In 1989, Mr. Skelton was inducted into the Academy of Television Arts and Sciences Hall of Fame. Then in 1990, at the age of 80 he gave a farewell performance at Carnegie Hall. His billing described him simply as " One of America's Clowns"

Clowns were always his fortune: in his spare time he did paintings of clown faces that fetched $80,000 and more. He once estimated that he earned $2.5 million a year from lithographs.

# *Final Resting Place*

Forest Lawn Memorial Park
1712 S. Glendale Ave
Glendale, CA 91025

*"Good night and God bless"*

## Dinah Shore

# 1917-1994

Dinah Shore died Thursday February 24, 1994 at her home in Beverly Hills, California from complications from ovarian cancer just a few days before her birthday. She had been diagnosed with ovarian cancer in 1993. She was 76.

Fannye Rose Shore was born on February 29, 1916 in Winchester, Tennessee. She graduated from Vanderbilt University and majored in sociology. It was from the WSM radio station theme song that she adopted her name "Dinah" then legally changed it in 1944

Dinah's career spanned more than 50 years, which included radio, recordings and television. She had 75 hit records between 1940 and 1955. In 1942 her recording of "Blue in the Night" sold a million copies. Her first number one hit in 1944 was "I'll Walk Alone," followed by "The Gypsy," "The Anniversary Song," "Buttons and Bows," and "Dear Hearts and Gentle People."

She had been honored with 10 Emmy Awards from her weekly television show, *The Dinah Shore Show* in November 1951. She also sang the jingle

"See the U.S.A. in Your Chevrolet" which became her unofficial theme. From 1970 to 1984, she was the host of several talk shows paving the way for other talk show stars like Oprah Winfrey.

She was married and divorced twice but it was her 6-year relationship with actor Burt Reynolds in the 70s that was highly publicized.

Shore was a longtime player and supporter of women's golf. In 1972 she founded the Colgate Dinah Shore Golf Tournament. She was an honorary member of the LPGA Hall of Fame.

## Celebration of Life

Funeral services were private. Memorial services were at 2 p.m. March 7th at the Directors Guild.

## Final Resting Place

Dinah was cremated the same day she died. Her ashes were divided and she has two burial sites. Half are at Hillside Memorial Park Cemetery in Culver City (LA), California. The other half is at Forest Lawn Cemetery (Cathedral City) Palm Springs, California.

Hillside Memorial Park
6001 W. Centinela Ave
Culver City, CA 90045

Forest Lawn Cemetery
(Cathedral City)
69855 Ramon Rd.
Palm Springs, CA 92234

## Carole Lombard

# 1908-1942

Carole Lombard died on January 16, 1942 in Mt. Potosi, Nevada after the plane she was riding in crashed. She was returning from a war bond tour. She had been advised to return to Hollywood by train due to weather and wartime fears. But Carole insisted on flying instead. The crash was surrounded by mystery as to why an experienced pilot crashed into the mountain? Gable rushed to the city, hoping for a miracle and then keeping a vigil until rescue teams recovered his wife's remains. Lombard, her mother, Gable's press agent and 19 other passengers and crew had exploded in a fireball only 20 minutes, after taking off from McCarran Field.

Jane Alice Peters was born on October 6, 1908 in Fort Wayne, Indiana. When she was six her parents separated and she moved to California. She was discovered by a movie scout playing stickball with the boys. As she moved up in the movie business she changed her name to Carole Lombard and soon she was an up and coming starlet. On June 26,1931 she married her costar, William Powell who was 16 years her senior. They divorced 2 years later. She was nominated for an Oscar in 1936 for her roll in *My Man Godfrey*. She also had a reputation for profane language.

Clark Gable was married when they became an item. They had a romance for 3 years before his divorce was granted on March 8, 1939. They eloped to Kingman, Arizona, where they were married March 29, 1939. The couple referred to each other as "Ma" and "Pa." The two were fond of gags and often tried to one-up the other one.

## Celebration of Life

Lombard's funeral was held on January 21 at Forest Lawn Memorial Park Cemetery in Glendale, California. Clark sat in the front pew and spoke to no one. He had purchased three crypts: one for Bessie, one for Carole and one for himself. Cariole had requested in her will that she be buried in a white dress. The dress was laid on top of what was left of her body in the coffin. After the funeral Clark became unapproachable.

## Final Resting Place

She was interred beside her mother under the name of
Carole Lombard Gable. Clark Gable is beside her.

# 1906-1975

Ozzie Nelson died at 4:30 a.m. on June 3, 1975 of liver cancer at his home in Hollywood, California. He was 69. He had suffered from recurring malignant tumors. His sons and wife were at his bedside.

Oswald George Nelson was born March 20, 1906 in New Jersey City, New Jersey. Ozzie began a musical career as a bandleader. He had his own band in the 30s and had a number one hit, "And Then Some." He married the band's vocalist, Hilliard, in October 1935. (Harriet)

They had two sons David and Ricky. Ozzie will always be known as the father on the hit TV show *The Adventures of Ozzie and Harriet.*

*The Adventures of Ozzie and Harriet* originated by Ozzie as a radio program that aired from 1944 - 1949. In 1952 it moved over to television and aired on television until 1966. Millions of fans watch as Ozzie raised his sons while producing and directing most of the episodes and co-writing many of them. Even though his character was a laid-back father...he was known as a workaholic. The younger audience had no idea that Ozzie and Harriet had previously been involved in music. But they did know their son, Ricky, as a musician and heartthrob.

Ozzie Nelson has two stars on the Hollywood Walk of Fame in Hollywood. One for his contribution to radio and one for television. Ozzie released his autobiography in 1973 and revealed that he was a lifelong atheist.

## Celebration of Life

A private service was held on Friday, June 6, 1975 at the Church of the Hills at Forest Lawn.

## Final Resting Place

Forest Lawn Hollywood Hills
6300 Forest Lawn Dr
Los Angeles, CA 90068

He was laid to rest in the Nelson family plot.

Del Wood (Queen of Ragtime pianist)

# 1920-1989

Del Wood died on October 3, 1989 at Baptist Hospital in Nashville, Tennesse following a stroke on September 22. She was 69.

Polly Adelaide Hendricks was born February 22, 1920 in Nashville, Tennessee. Her parents gave her a piano for her fifth birthday. Although her parents wanted her to be a classical pianist she preferred honky-tonk music. Being raised in Nashville her dream was to perform on the Grand Ole Opry

When she was 20 she started playing in bands and honky-tonk joints and shortened her name to Del. It was while she was playing as a staff pianist at WLBJ in Bowling Green, Kentucky that her music got recognized. In 1951 "Down Yonder" soon became a national hit both in pop and country. It sold over 1 million copies. She was one of the first female country solo instrumentalist to sell a million records. That led to her many appearances on the Grand Ole Opry.

In 1968 Wood was part of one of the Grand Ole Opry package tours that entertained troupes overseas. In 1973 Jerry Lee Lewis performed on the Grand

Ole Opry and called Del out on the stage to perform her hit "Down Yonder" with him. In 1984 she made a cameo appearance in the film "Rhinestone," featuring Dolly Parton and Sylvester Stallone.

Dell continued to play on the Grand Ole Opry until just before her death.

## Final Resting Place

Mount Olive Cemetery
1101 Lebanon Pike
Nashville, TN 37210

## Richard Crenna

## 1926-2003

Richard Crenna died Friday at 6 p.m. at Cedars Sinai Medical Center in Los Angeles, California. Crenna had pancreatic cancer and died of heart failure with his wife and children by his side. He was 76.

Richard Donald Crenna was born November 30, 1926 in Los Angeles, California. At the age of 10, he played a squeaky-voiced kid on the *Burns and Allen* radio show. After he served in the Army during World War II he was cast again with a squeaky-voiced teenager Walter on the radio comedy *Our Miss Brooks* with Eve Arden. When the show moved to television in 1952 he began working between television and films. He appeared in over 115 films during his career.

From 1957-1963 he starred beside Walter Brennan in the long-running CBS series The Real McCoys. From 1966-1984 he played in some great films that included the *Sand Pebbles, Wait Until Dark, Body Heat* and *The Flamingo Kid*. His favorite role was Colonel Sam Trautman in the *Rambo* film trilogy. Crenna was a regular on several TV Series and enjoyed directing. He directed episodes of the TV series *The Rockford Files, The Andy Grifffith Show* and *Lou Grant*.

# Celebration of Life

There was a private funeral and public memorial service Saturday, January 25. In lieu of flowers, the family requests that donations be made to the Cedars-Sinai Comprehensive Cancer Center.

# Final Resting Place

Crenna was cremated and his ashes were given to his family.

Richard Crenna was inducted to the Walk of Fame on May 23, 1988.

# Dobie Gray

# 1940-2011

Dobie Gray died Tuesday, December 6, 2011 in Nashville, Tennessee from complications of cancer surgery. He was 71.

Lawrence Darrow Brown could have been his birth name but also Leonard Victor Ainsworth. And his birth could have been in 1940, 1942, or 1943. He was born into a sharecropper family outside of Houston, either Brookshire or Simonton, Texas. Gray's early life is not well documented. However his interest in music came from his Baptist minister grandfather.

Gray left Texas in the 60s for Los Angeles where he got work with Sonny Bono. In 1963 he had his first hit, "Look At Me." It was then that he changed his name to Dobie Gray. His musical talent ranged from soul, country, pop and musical theater. Among a variety of recording successes he also contributed to movie soundtracks. He spent 2 ½ years acting in the production "Hair" in Los Angeles.

In the 70s he joined a band that was managed by "Jethro" of the Beverly Hillbillies. But it was when he won a recording contract with Decca Records in 1972 that he traveled to Nashville and worked with Mentor Williams. He recorded "Drift Away" which became a cross over hit and his signature song written by Williams.

Gray also penned some huge songs recorded by some great recording artists that include John Conlee ("Got My Heart Set on You"), Ray Charles ("Over and Over, Again"), Julio Iglesias ("If I Ever Needed You") and George Jones ("Come Home to Me").

In the mid 80s he re-launched his recording career and had two singles on the US country chart, "That's One to Grow On" which peaked at #35. His country albums included *From Where I Stand* in 1986. He also recorded TV advertising jingles for companies including Budweiser, Coca-Cola, Chevrolet and McDonald's.

He returned to the US charts for the last time in 2003, when he appeared on a remake of "Drift Away," singing with the rap-rock star Uncle Kracker.

## Celebration of Life

There was a public visitation at Woodlawn Roesch-Patton Funeral Home from 3 p.m. until 8 p.m. Wednesday, December 14, 2011.

A public funeral service was held at 2:00 p.m. on Thursday, December 15, 2011 at Brentwood Baptist Church, 7777 Concord Road, Brentwood, TN 37027.

Gray, who was not married and had no children, willed much of his property and future earnings to St. Jude Children's Research Hospital in Memphis, TN.

In lieu of customary floral tributes, memorials may be made to St. Jude Children's Research Hospital, 501 St. Jude Place, Memphis, TN 38105.

# Final Resting Place

Woodlawn Memorial Park
660 Thompson Lane
Nashville, TN 37204

# 1921-1992

Chuck Connors died on November 10, 1992 at Cedars-Sinai Medical Center in Los Angeles, California of pneumonia due to lung cancer. He was a heavy smoker and was 71 years old.

Kevin Joseph Connors was born April 10, 1921 in Brooklyn, New York. His parents were immigrants from Newfoundland and were from Irish decent. He was a natural athlete and during high school and college it earned him scholarships to attend private schools. He was in the army from 1942-1946. Baseball was his first love, which he pursued after the army.

For several years Connors played professional sports, both basketball and baseball teams including the Dodgers, Cubs and Celtics. In 1952 while with the Los Angeles Angels, a casting director for MGM saw him and recommended he audition for a part in a movie, Spencer Tracy-Katharine Hepburn's comedy, *Pat and Mike*. He got the part and then devoted his attention to a full time acting career. His 6'5" physique seemed to help him with rugged acting roles.

He appeared in over 45 movies and numerous television series and specials. He was nominated for an Emmy Award for his role as a slave owner in the mini-series *Roots* and also won a Golden Globe Award in 1959. But it was the hit TV show *The Rifleman* that aired from 1958-1963 that made him famous. His character was the sharpshooting good guy and devoted father, Lucas McCain. McCain toted around a nifty modified Winchester Model 1892 with a big ring lever, which allowed him to cock the gun by spinning it in his left hand. It became his trademark on the show.

Connors was inducted into the Cowboy Hall of Fame in 1991.

## Celebration of Life

Johnny Crawford who portrayed Chuck Connors' on-screen son, delivered a famous eulogy at Chuck's funeral, commemorating the time he spent with the deceased actor. Johnny continued to praise his former co-star long after he passed away saying, "He was very gregarious and friendly, and not at all bashful. It was a good experience for me to spend time with Chuck and learn how he dealt with people. I learned a great deal from him about acting, and he was a tremendous influence on me. He was just my hero."

# Final Resting Place

San Fernando Mission Cemetery
11160 Stranwood Ave
Mission Hills, CA 91345

His tombstone has a photo of him as Lucas McCain in *The Rifleman* and also logos of the baseball teams he played for: the Dodgers, Celtics and Cubs.

The Singing Brakeman.

## Jimmy Rodgers

## 1897-1933

Jimmy Rodgers died of tuberculosis on May 26, 1933 at the Taft Hotel in New York. Rodgers knew his death was coming and actually sang about it. Tuberculosis was a common killer in those days and his health was declining. So he took a train to New York to record what proved to be his final recording session for RCA. His health had deteriorated so much that he had to rest on a cot between sessions and at times had to be propped up to record. He was 35.

Jimmie Rodgers was born James Charles Rodgers outside Meridian, Mississippi, on September 8, 1897. He taught himself to play the guitar while working around the railroad and learned to sing in church. He won an amateur talent show when he was 13. From age fourteen until he was twenty-eight, he worked, sometimes irregularly, as a brakeman or flagman on railroads.

In 1924 he contracted tuberculosis and discovered that railroad work made it hard for him to breathe, so Rodgers started singing in traveling shows, vaudeville shows, medicine shows, and various other production. Around 1927 he joined a group called Tenneva Ramblers from Bristol, Tennessee and had a weekly show on a new radio station, WWNC in Ashville. The show was called *The Jimmy Rodgers Entertainers*.

Rogers got his big break in Bristol, Tennessee when he performed two songs during an audition. "Sleep, Baby, Sleep" and "The Soldier's Sweetheart." Rodgers went into the studio the next day and made a recording which quickly introduced him to a national audience for the first time. Rodgers was more determined than ever to be an entertainer and was very busy following his dream. He did a movie for Columbia Pictures, *The Singing Brakeman* and did a tour with humorist Will Rogers. He continued to write and record during his six-year career. He recorded more than 100 songs.

Rodgers' most notable musical innovation was 13 series of songs he called *Blue Yodels*. In 1930 he recorded "Blue Yodel No. 9" with Louis Armstrong on trumpet. The series became so popular that Yodeling became Rodgers trademark. By 1932 Rodgers gave up touring because of his health but he continued on a weekly radio show in San Antonio, Texas.

He was the first performer inducted into the Country Music Hall of Fame in 1961. On May 24, 1978, the United States Postal Service issued a 13-cent commemorative stamp honoring Rodgers.

## Celebration of Life

On Monday, May 29. 1933, mourners viewed the body of Rodgers at the Scottish Rite Cathedral until 4:00 p.m. His body was taken to the Central Methodist Church in Meridian, Mississippi for funeral services.

# Final Resting Place

Oak Grove Cemetery
680 Oak Grove Drive
Meridian, MS 39301

# 1922-1969

Judy Garland died on June 22, 1969, twelve days after her 47th birthday. She was found dead in her home in London, England. After an autopsy it was believed she died from an overdose of barbiturates, but not a suicide.

Frances Ethel Gumm was born June 10, 1922 in Grand Rapids, Minnesota. Her family relocated to California in 1926. She began performing in vaudeville with her two older sisters when she was a teenager. It was during that time the sisters decided to change their names to Garland.

A few days after a scout heard the sisters, Judy was signed to a contract with MGM. She was 14 years old. During her career Garland made more than two dozen films. Nine of them were with Mickey Rooney. Her most famous role was in 1939 as Dorothy in *The Wizard of Oz*. Other outstanding films were *Meet Me in St Louis* made in 1944, *The Harvey Girls* made in 1946, and *Easter Parade* in 1948.

In 1963 she début her own television series, *The Judy Garland Show* but it was cancelled after 26 episodes. The show was nominated for four Emmy Awards.

She received many special awards during her career. In 1999, the American Film Institute placed her among the 10 greatest female stars of classic American cinema.

While her career was amazingly successful her personal life suffered. From a young teenager the pressure of stardom continued to affect her physical and mental health. Drugs and alcohol led to her death.

## Celebration of Life

Her body had been embalmed and taken to New York City on June 26, where an estimated 20,000 people lined up to pay their respects at the Frank E. Campbell Funeral Chapel in Manhattan. The funeral home remained open all night long to accommodate the overflow crowd as they strolled by her glass-enclosed casket.

On June 27, there was an Episcopal service let by the Rev. Peter A. Delaney of St Marylebone Parish Church, London, who had officiated at her marriage to Deans, three months prior. The celebrity list included Lauren Bacall, Mickey Rooney, and James Mason who delivered the eulogy.

## Final Resting Place

Hollywood Forever Cemetery
6000 Santa Monica Blvd
Los Angeles, CA

She was interred in a crypt in the community mausoleum at Ferncliff Cemetery in Hartsdale, New York, a small town 24 miles north of midtown Manhattan. At the request of her children, Garland's remains were removed from Ferncliff Cemetery in January 2017 and relocated 2,800 miles away at the Hollywood Forever Cemetery in Los Angeles.

## Luther Perkins

## 1928-1968

Luther Perkins died on August 5, 1968 from a house fire. He was 40. Perkins had gone fishing earlier that morning and returned to his den to relax. He fell asleep in a chair with a cigarette in his hand, which he often did, and accidentally starting a fire. His daughter, who had been sleeping, found the den and kitchen full of smoke and a blaze. A neighbor helped his wife and daughter pull an unconscious Perkins from the house. He was taken to Vanderbilt University Hospital where Johnny Cash met them. He never regained consciousness and died with over 50 percent of his body burned.

Luther Monroe Perkins was born January 8, 1928 in Como, Mississippi. He was the son of a Baptist preacher and taught himself to play the guitar. He started his career while working with Roy Cash at an automobile sales company in Memphis. They would bring their guitars to work and play together when work was slow. In 1954 Roy Cash introduced his brother, Johnny Cash.

In 1954 Perkins joined Johnny Cash for an audition with Sun Records and became his guitarist for the rest of his career.

Cash and Perkins often interacted on stage joking around proving the signature "boom-check-a-boom" background sound. His creatively simple, sparsely embellished, rhythmic use of Fender Esquire, Jazz master and Jaguar guitars made him an iconic guitarist and well known for his rockabilly music.

He was inducted into the Rockabilly Hall of Fame. When the movie "Walk the Line" was released in 2005 there was a scene showing Perkins asleep in a chair with a lit cigarette hanging in his mouth. Joaquin Phoenix, who portrayed Cash, removes the burning cigarette and stubs it out in a nearby ashtray.

Perkins' nickname was "L.M.," the initials of his first and second name "Luther Monroe." Singer-guitarist Carl Perkins, who was also a member of Cash's touring show, was not related to Luther Perkins.

## *Final Resting Place*

Hendersonville Memory Gardens
353 Main Street
Hendersonville, TN 37075

Luther was buried on August 7, 1968. Pallbearers were Johnny Cash, Roger Miller and Marshall Grand. Before Luther's casket was lowered into the grave, Cash was overheard saying "Thank You, Luther." He was buried in the same cemetery where Cash had bought a series of plots for his own family.

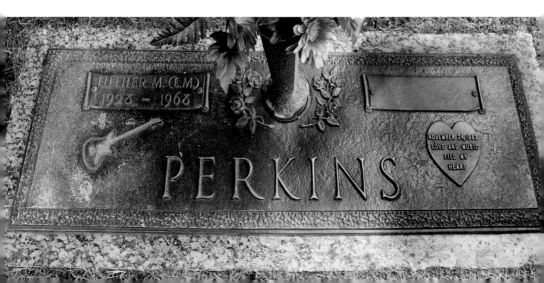

Randy Hughes was the fourth person killed in the crash that took the lives of Patsy Cline, Hawkshaw Hawkins and Cowboy Copas on March 5, 1963. He was 34.

Hughes was the pilot and Cline's manager. He was married to Kathy Copas, the daughter of Cowboy Copas.

Ramsey Dorris Hughes was born September 11, 1928 in Gum, Tennessee. He was a highly respected Nashville session guitarist playing for several country music artists including Cowboy Copas. After deciding that he could do more than just play a guitar in a country band, he made a career change to managing country artist's careers. In 1959, Patsy Cline became one of his clients. After taking basic flying lessons, he purchased a yellow Piper PA-24 Comanche to fly his clients from one show to another. He reasoned that purchasing the plane would be to his client's advantage; they would arrive faster for their performances, thus not have to depend on slower cars for transportation.

In March 1963, Cline had been trying to get back home to Nashville from a benefit concert in Kansas City. Instead of traveling by car she chose to fly with her manager the 500 miles by plane with his father-in-law, Cowboy Copas and Hawkshaw Hawkins. Randy phoned his wife in Tennessee and learned that "the storm had passed." He gave her his flight plan to hop from one small airport to another, while waiting for storms to clear the area before taking off for the next short haul.

With radio contact and a flight plan the four left Kansas City at approximately 2 pm and then landed at the Rogers, Arkansas airport to refuel and check the weather. They then left for Dyersburg and landed at the Dyersburg, Tennessee airport around 5:05 p.m. Randy asked for a weather briefing for the final leg to Nashville. He was told weather conditions were marginal. The group had the chance to stay free overnight at the local motel there but declined the offer. Hughes told aviation officials he would try the flight and return if the weather conditions worsened.

The passengers and Hughes reloaded the Piper Comanche. Hughes requested another weather briefing by radio then taxied into position and took off at 6:07 p.m.

No further radio contact was made with aviation officials. At 6:29 p.m. the aircraft crashed in a swampy wooded area one mile north of highway 70 and five miles west of Camden. Investigators believe that Hughes entered an area of worsening weather with low visibility and lost his visual reference with the ground. This induced spatial disorientation and eventually led to a graveyard spiral with the aircraft entering into a right-hand diving turn, with a nose-down altitude. When the aircraft cleared the clouds, Hughes probably attempted to arrest the high descent rate by pulling the nose up and applying full power, but it was too late. The FAA investigators later found evidence that the propeller was at maximum speed during impact at approximately 175 miles per hour.

Hughes held a valid private pilot license with an airplane single-engine land rating, but was not rated to fly under instrument flight rules. Hughes had taken possession of the airplane in 1962, less than a year before the crash, and was an inexperienced pilot with a total flight time of 160:10 hours including 44:25 logged in the Piper Comanche.

# Celebration of Life

Randy's casket was third in line of the four caskets. Each one had their photos on top. The memorial service was held at Phillips-Robinson Funeral Home in Nashville, Tennessee, on the morning of March 8, 1963 with his father-in-law, Cowboy Copas.

## Final Resting Place

Forest Lawn Memorial Gardens
1150 Dickerson Rd
Goodlettsville, TN 37072

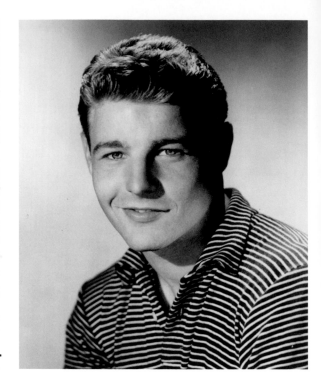

## Dave Nelson

## 1936-2011

THE ADVENTURES OF *Ozzie and Harriet*

D ave Nelson, who played the oldest son on the 1950's TV show *The Adventures of Ozzie and Harriet* died on January 11, 2011 at his, Century City, California home, from complications stemming from colon cancer. He was 74 and the final member of the Nelson family to pass away.

David Oswald Nelson was born on October 24, 1936 in New York City. His family moved to Los Angeles, CA where he attended High School and College. *The Adventures of Ozzie and Harriet* TV show was actually filmed in the family's real Hollywood Hills home and the show was based on the real family. It ran from 1952 to 1966.

David and his brother, Rick both starred as themselves in the long running TV series. When they were in High School the show portrayed them in High School. When they enrolled in college the show portrayed them in college. When they both married in the 60s, their spouses also became members of the cast. It became apparent that the fans were unclear at times as to what was real and what was not real.

David in real life did not follow his TV character into Law but became a director and TV producer. David directed and produced several episodes of *The Adventures of Ozzie and Harriet* during the 16-years it was on the air. Nelson continued acting in several movies between 1957-1965 including *Peyton Place*, *The Big Circus*, *Day of the Outlaw*, *Hondo* and *Swing Out*. His television roles included *The Love Boat*, *Last Plane Out*, *Goodnight Beantown*, and *A Rare Breed*. He was awarded a star on the Hollywood Walk of frame in 1996.

## Celebration of Life

Nelson's private funeral was at noon on Thursday, January 13, 2011 at Westwood Memorial Park.

## Final Resting Place

Westwood Village Memorial Park
1218 Glendon Ave
Los Angeles, CA 90024

David was cremated and not buried in the family plot in Forest Lawn Memorial Park in Hollywood Hills; instead he chose Westwood Memorial Park's outdoor Garden of Serenity columbarium.

DAVID OZZIE NELSON

1936 – 2011

OUR DARLING

HUSBAND AND FATHER

HAS GONE FISHING

1903-1952

Curly Howard died January 18, 1952 from serious health problems resulting from multiple strokes. He was 48.

Jerome Lest Horwitz was born October 22, 1903 in Brooklyn, New York. He was the brother of Moe and Shemp who made up the comedy team, The Three Stooges and youngest of five brothers. He was nicknamed "Babe" by his brothers. He was a quiet child who never finished high school, but he was an accomplished ballroom dancer and singer. He idolized his brothers and hung around backstage at performances.

It wasn't until Shemp left that Moe suggested Curly fill the role. Everyone thought he was too handsome with a head of hair and thick mustache and not funny looking. Curly left the room and returning with his head shaved. It was from the comment

"Boy, don't you look girlie?" that was misunderstood as "Boy, don't you look curly?" that became the perfect name. Curly became an integral part of The Three Stooges.

He was known for his high-pitch voice and vocal expression "nyuk-nyuk-nyuk!" and barking like a dog and "indestructible" head. His hulking frame bursting out of a too-small suite was irredeemably incompetent man-child, the knucklehead and recipient of most of Moe's abuse – zany punches, slaps, smackes and bonks on the head. Curly was so good at improv that many times in their movies, directors would simply let the camera roll freely as Curly did his thing. If he forgot his lines he just added "Womb, woob, woob" and continued the scene uninterrupted.

List of Curly Words and Expressions:

*"Nyuk, nyuk, nyuk"* – Curly's traditional laughter, accompanied by manic finger-snapping, often used to amuse himself

*"Woob, woob, woob!"* – used when he was either scared, dazed, or flirting with a "dame;"

*"Hmmm!"* – an under-the-breath, high-pitched sound meant to show different emotions, including interest, excitement, frustration, or anger; one of his most-used reactions/expressions;

*"Nyahh-ahhh-ahhh!"* – scared reaction (this was the reaction most often used by the other Stooges after Curly's departure),

*"Laaa-Deeeeeee"* or simply *"Laaa, laaa, laaa"* – Curly's working "song"; also used when he was acting innocently right before taking out an enemy;

*"Ruff Ruff"* – dog bark, used to give an enemy a final push before departing the scene, or barking at an attractive dame;

*"Ha-cha-cha-cha-cha!"* – a take on Jimmy Durante's famed call, used more sparingly than other expressions;

*"I'm a victim of soicumstance [circumstance]"*;

*"Soiteny!"* ("certainly");

*"I'll moider you!"* ("I'll murder you!"; used as a threat, but much more by Moe than by Curly);

*"Huff huff huff!"* – sharp, huffing exhales either due to excitement or meant to provoke a foe;

*"Ah-ba-ba-ba-ba-ba-ba!"* – used during his later years, a sort of nonsense, high-pitched yelling that signified being scared or overly excited;

*"Indubitably"* – an expression used to feign an intelligent response;

Curly's teeth, while chattering nervously, made the sound of a small hammer striking a chisel;

*"A WISE Guy, Eh?"* – annoyed response;

Curly loved dogs and often picked up strays when they were traveling. He would take them from town to town with him until he found them a home somewhere else on the tour.

It's been claimed that Curly invented break dancing. In times of stress he would fall to the ground and run in a circle using his shoulder as a pivot.

Curly left the Three Stooges act in 1946 after having a massive stroke. He had another stroke in 1948 that left him partially paralyzed. However... the bright side was that he met and married his wife and they had a baby daughter in 1948. As his health deteriorated he was placed in a nursing home in 1951, where he suffered another stroke. As his mental state worsened he was moved several times for immediate care before he died.

## Celebration of Life

He was given a private Jewish funeral.

# Final Resting Place

Home of Peace Memorial Park
4334 Whittier Blvd
Los Angeles, CA 90023

# 1919-1991

Tennessee Ernie Ford died Thursday, October 17, 1991 at HCA Hospital in Reston, Virginia of liver failure from alcoholism. He got sick at the Dulles International Airport after attending a state dinner at the White House on September 28th and was rushed to the hospital. Although he'd suffered two previous attacks years before, this was fatal. He was 72.

Ernest Jennings Ford was born February 13, 1919 in Bristol, Tennessee.

In high school he sang in school productions and in a glee club. Ford spent most his spare time at the local radio station and was hired as a disc jockey after high school. He served in the Army Air Forces during World War II as a B-29 bomber navigator. After the service he moved to Pasadena, California as a hillbilly disc jockey and newscaster. He obtained a record deal after performing on *Hometown Jamboree* as a soloist. His first country hits were "Mule Train" and "Smokey Mountain Boogie."

Ford hosted *The Ford Show*, a prime time variety show named after the sponsor, Ford Motor Company, which ran from 1956-1961.

His recording released in 1955, "Sixteen Tons" which sold more than 20 million copies made him a house hold name as a singer. He recorded more than 80 albums and sold more than 24 million albums. He received a Grammy in 1964 for his album "Great Gospel Songs."

Ford was also known for his phrases "Bless your pea-pickin' hearts" and "Nervous as a long-tailed cat in a roomful of rockin' chairs."

## Celebration of Life

A military funeral was held on Monday, October 21, 1991 with an honor guard in Pala Alto, California. Family, friends, musicians and Air Force buddies packed in the church to pay tribute and praise Ford's talents. His songs "Sixteen Tons" and the "Ballad of Davy Crockett" were honored by TV viewers across America.

## Final Resting Place

Alta Mesa Memorial Park
695 Arastradero Rd
Palo Alto, CA 94306

Carroll O'Connor

# 1924-2001

Carroll O'Connor died Thursday, June 21, 2001 from a heart attack brought on by complications from diabetes. He was 76.

Carroll O' Connor was born on August 2, 1924, in Manhattan, New York City. During World War II, he joined the merchant marine as a teen and sailed on 14 ships as a purser. After the war he attended college and was cast in a play. He decided to accompany his brother to Ireland where he started appearing in plays at the Gate Theater. In 1952 after returning to the States he began his professional acting career.

Carroll O'Connor was mainly known for his stage work and a few small movie roles before playing Archie Bunker on the hit TV series *All In the Family*. He had been living in Europe when approached about the role. He accepted on the condition that he would have a return airplane ticket back to Rome when the show failed. Instead it became the highest rated television on American television for five consecutive seasons during the 1971-1979 run. O'Connor was nominated for eight Emmy Awards as Outstanding Lead Actor in a Comedy Series and won four times.

When *All In the Family* ended, *Archie Bunker's Place* continued in its place. The show was canceled in 1983. In March of 1988 he starred in a new sitcom *In the Heat of the Night* based on the 1967 movie of the same name. In 1989, while working on the set, he was hospitalized and had to undergo open-heart surgery causing him to miss several seasons. However he won his fifth Emmy Award as Police Chief Bill Gillespie.

In 1995 tragedy struck O'Connor. His only child, Hugh, who was his co-star in the TV series, shot himself in a drug-related suicide. Carroll began traveling throughout the United States promoting new laws that allow families of drug abuse victims to sue drug dealers for monetary damages. Thirteen states passed such a law, including New York, California and Illinois.

## Celebration of Life

Hundreds attended the funeral for O'Connor held at St. Paul the Apostle Roman Catholic Church in West Los Angeles. Celebrities who attended were *All In The Family* cast members Carl Reiner, Sally Struthers, and Danielle Brisebois, as well as producer Norman Lear. Jean Stapleton was not able to make the service. Others who attended were Don Rickles, Larry Hagman, and Richard Crenna, Alan Autry, Denise Nicholas, and Martin Sheen.

Cardinal Mahoney, the archbishop of Los Angeles, presided over the traditional Catholic Mass. Larry Hagman and Martin Sheen performed Scripture readings. For the finale there were was a final standing ovation as 76 doves were released to represent every year of the actor's life.

# Final Resting Place

Westwood Village Memorial Park
1218 Glendon Ave
Los Angeles, CA 90024

## Roy Orbison

## 1936-1988

Roy Orbison died on Tuesday night December 6, 1988 of a heart attack at his mother's home in Hendersonville, Tennessee. He was taken by ambulance to the hospital after spending the day with country singer Jean Shepard's family. Orbinson often stopped by Nashville to visit his mother after a performance if he was near by. He was 52.

Roy Kelton Orbison was born April 23, 1936 in Vernon, Texas. His parents gave him his first guitar when he was six and by the age of eight he was performing on the radio. In high school he sang in a rockabilly and country band. While attending North Texas State College his classmate, Pat Boone, encourage him to go into the recording studio. Roy and his band continued to perform at dances and TV shows until they finally got a record deal. They recorded a rockabilly song called "Ooby Dooby" for Sun Records in 1956 and it hit the charts selling over 200,000 copies. Roy and his band *The Teen Kings* toured with Sonny James, Johnny Horton, Carl Perkins, and Cash. The band soon disbanded but Orbison stayed in Memphis and continued to write.

During the 1960s Orbison had 22 Top 40 hits in less than five years, however, there was personal tragedy. In 1966 after moving to Nashville, his wife, Claudette was killed while they were riding motorcycles. Two years later two of his young sons were killed in a house fire.

Roy found himself unable to write songs for a while, but maintained a positive outlook and continued touring.

In 1977 Linda Ronstadt recorded "Blue Bayou," and not long after Don McLean had a hit with his 1980 cover of "Crying." In 1982 hard rockers Van Halen recorded "Pretty Woman," which showed up again in the 1990 Richard Gere/Julia Roberts movie of the same name.

Orbison was inducted into the Rock and Roll Hall of Fame (by Springsteen), the Nashville Songwriters Hall of Fame, and the Songwriters Hall of Fame. He is 13th on Rolling Stone's list of the 100 Greatest Singers of All Time and in 2002, Billboard magazine listed Orbison No. 74 in the Top 600 recording artists.

## Celebration of Life

A memorial was held in Nashville, and another in Los Angeles.

# *Final Resting Place*

Westwood Village Memorial Park
1218 Glendon Ave
Los Angeles, CA 90024

Roy is buried in an unmarked grave. The Orbison's family had originally said they planned to install an elaborate, black granite headstone, inscribed with the singer's songs - but his grave remains without a marker. I placed a flower where his grave is located, which is close to TV Host Richard Dawson.

The Final Resting places of Orbison's wife, two sons, brother and mother are all located together at
Woodlawn Memorial Park
660 Thompson Lane
Nashville, TN 37204

# 1928-1996

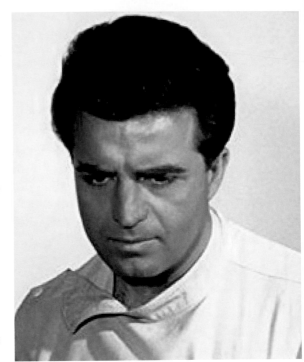

Vince Edwards died Monday night, March 11, 1996 of pancreatic cancer at UCLA medical Center in Los Angeles, California. He was 67. Edwards had been hospitalized 11 days prior.

Vince Edward Zoine was born July 9, 1928 in Brooklyn, New York. He and his twin was the youngest of seven children. Edwards studied aviation mechanics in high school but it was his athletic ability that landed him a scholarship to Ohio State College. He left early to live in Hawaii and train as a swimmer for the Olympics but because of health issues he returned to New York to study acting.

He made his Broadway debut in 1947 in *High Button Shoes*. In 1951 he signed a contract with Paramount Pictures and began acting in a few B pictures. He did get noticed for his small role in *The Three Faces of Eve* in 1957. His big break in 1961 and kind of by accident. When Edwards arrived for his audition, he went into the wrong audition room. Instead of reading for a role as an airline pilot, he read for the part of a young doctor, Dr. Ben Casey. His role in the TV show *Ben Casey* made him a star overnight. The show ran for five years and rated in the top ten during the 1962-63 season. Edwards' interest in directing also gave him the opportunity to direct a few of the episodes that ran from 1961-1966.

Edwards did make TV history by showing his chest hair underneath his unbuttoned scrubs, which was a TV taboo.

And he used the show to launch a singing career, recording six albums, including *Vince Edwards Sings*, and playing Las Vegas

In the later years Edwards went on to direct episodes of the *Mike Hammer* series for CBS as well as episodes of *Fantasy Island, Police Story,* and *In The Heat of the Night.* In 1988, he made the syndicated TV movie *The Return of Ben Casey.* However his compulsive gambling kept him from pursuing further success.

## Celebration of Life

In September Edwards received a memorial tribute at the Emmy's.

## Final Resting Place

Private services for the actor was held on Friday in Los Angeles.

Holly Cross Cemetery
5835 West Slauson Ave.
Culver City, CA 90230

Jimmy Stewart

# Jimmy Stewart

## 1908-1997

J immy Stewart died Wednesday, July 2, 1997 at his home in Los Angeles from a blood clot in his lung. He was 89.

James Maitland Stewart was born on May 20, 1908, in Indiana, Pennsylvania. As a young boy he worked on model airplanes in his basement and dreamed of becoming an airline pilot. His musical talents began with him learning the accordion. He graduated in 1932 from Princeton Academy. While in school he became interested in the school's drama and music clubs and performed with a summer stock company. After summer stock he moved to New York and roomed with Henry Fonda while performing on Broadway. With Fonda's encouragement, Stewart went to Los Angeles and agreed to take a screen test, after which he signed a contract with MGM in April 1935, as a contract player for up to seven years at $350 a week. He then starred in dozens of films. Not forgetting his first love, he gained his private pilot certificate in 1935 and commercial pilot license in 1938.

Stewart also had a noted military career and was a World War II and Vietnam War veteran and pilot, who rose to the rank of Brigadier General in the

United States Air Force Reserve, becoming the highest-ranking actor in military history.

From the beginning of Stewart's film career in 1935, through his final theatrical project in 1991, he appeared in more than 92 films, television programs and shorts. Five of his movies were included on the American Film Institute's list of the 100 greatest American films: *Mr. Smith Goes to Washington*; *The Philadelphia Story*; *It's a Wonderful Life*; *Rear Window* and *Vertigo*. His roles in *Mr. Smith Goes to Washington*, *The Philadelphia Story*, *It's a Wonderful Life*, *Harvey*, and *Anatomy of a Murder* earned him Academy Award nominations—with one win for *The Philadelphia Story*.

He received an Academy Lifetime Achievement award in 1985. In 1999, Stewart was named the third-greatest male screen legend of the Golden Age of Hollywood by the American Film Institute, behind Humphrey Bogart and Cary Grant.

## Celebration of Life

Over 3000 mourners, mostly celebrities, attended Stewart's memorial service. Jimmy Stewart's daughter Kelly Harcourt spoke at his funeral in Beverly Hills. She reminded mourners of the message of her father's favorite movie, *It's a Wonderful Life*: No man is poor who has friends. "Here's to our father," she said, "the richest man in town."

Forest Lawn Memorial Park
1712 S. Glendale Ave
Glendale, CA 91025

He's buried in a plot on the top of a hill close to the
Wee Kirk O' the Heather church.

"FOR HE SHALL GIVE HIS ANGELS CHARGE
OVER THEE TO KEEP THEE IN ALL THY WAYS"

## Ray Charles
## 1930-2004

Ray Charles died at 11:30 a.m. on Thursday, June 10, 2004 at his home in Beverly Hills, California of complications resulting from acute liver disease. He was surrounded by his family and friends. He was 73. His health deteriorated rapidly over the past year, after he had hip replacement surgery and was diagnosed with a failing liver.

Ray Charles Robinson was born September 23, 1930, in Albany, Ga. He showed interest in the piano at age three and was taught to play at local café. Ray started to lose his sight at around 4 or 5 years old as a result of glaucoma and was completely blind by age seven. He attended a blind school from 1937-1945. He continued piano learning to read music in Braille. His mother died when he was 14 and he moved to Florida living with friends and began playing not only the piano but also the saxophone in bands. His music talent spanned soul, rock'n'roll, R &B, country, jazz, big band and blues. He dropped his last name, Robinson.

His first big hit was 1959's "What'd I Say," a song built off a simple piano riff with suggestive moaning from the Raeletts. Some U.S. radio stations banned the song, but Charles was on his way to stardom.

Ray Charles had many friends in country music. Marty Stuart said "He made inroads for all of us when he did 'I Can't Stop Loving You.' It took country music to places it hadn't been before."

"I lost one of my best friends and I will miss him a lot," Willie Nelson.

Charles won nine of his 12 Grammy Awards between 1960 and 1966, including the best R&B recording three consecutive years ("Hit the Road Jack," "I Can't Stop Loving You" and "Busted").

Charles was no angel. His womanizing was legendary, and he struggled with a heroin addiction for nearly 20 years before quitting cold turkey in 1965.

His final album, *Genius Loves Company,* released two months after his death, consists of duets with various admirers and contemporaries: B. B. King, Van Morrison, Willie Nelson, James Taylor, Gladys Knight, Michael McDonald, Natalie Cole, Elton John, Bonnie Raitt, Diana Krall, Norah Jones and Johnny Mathis. The album won eight Grammy Awards.

At the time of his death he was survived by 12 children, 20 grandchildren and five great-grandchildren.

## Celebration of Life

A 2-hour funeral service took place on June 18, 2004, at the First African Methodist Episcopal Church in Los Angeles. Charles' son, the Rev. Robert Robinson Sr. and the Rev. Jesse Jackson started the service with hand clapping and reading from the Old Testament. Willy Nelson performed "Georgia On My Mind," with B. B. King, Glen Campbell, Stevie Wonder and Wynton Marsalis each paying tribute at the funeral. Another tribute came from Clint Eastwood who praised Charles as a genius. The funeral ended with the casket being opened and hundreds of mourners passing by as a recording of his "Somewhere Over the Rainbow" with Johnny Mathis. Other celebrities who attended were Little Richard, Cicely Tyson, Steven Segal, and Quincy Jones.

# Final Resting Place

Inglewood Park Cemetery
720 E Florence Ave
Inglewood, CA 90302

# 1927-2011

Peter Falk died peacefully on the evening of June 23, 2011 at his home in Beverly Hills, California. He was 83. Falk had Alzheimer's disease since 2007.

Peter Michael Falk was born September 16, 1927 in New York. He had his right eye removed at the age of three because of a tumor and wore a glass eye. Before he began his acting career he joined the Merchant Marine as a cook. He had a degree in political science and a master's degree in public administration. In 1956 he moved to New York and started appearing in many different plays on Broadway. He then switch to television and acted in several TV series like *Have Gun Will Travel, Wagon Train,* and *The Untouchables.* In 1958 his big-screen debut came in *Wind Across the Everglades.* He was twice nominated for a best supporting actor Oscar in 1960 for *Murder Inc.* and *Pocketful of Miracles.*

His most famous role was the trench coat wearing, cigar-smoking Lieutenant Columbo in the long-running television series, *Columbo.*

It aired from 1968 to 2003. He was known for uttering his catchphrase: 'Just one more thing" as he hung out at crime scenes. He won four Emmy's for his role as the iconic cop Lt. Columbo.

Falk was awarded a Star on the Hollywood Walk of Fame on July 25, 2013.

## Celebration of Life

There was a service held a Westwood Memorial Park.

## Final Resting Place

Westwood Memorial Park
1218 Glendon Ave
Los Angeles, CA 90024

SEPT 16, 1927     JUNE 23, 2011

PETER FALK

I'M NOT HERE
I'M HOME WITH SHERA

## Dottie Rambo

# 1943-1997

Dottie Rambo died on Mother's Day, Sunday, May 11, 2008 when her tour bus ran off the highway and hit an embankment in Missouri. She was 74.

Joyce Reba Lutrell was born on March 2, 1934 in Madison, Kentucky. She started writing songs at the age of 8 and was singing and playing guitar on local country radio at 10. Her musical direction changed from country music to singing gospel music when she gave her heart to Christ at 12 years old. When she was 16 she married Buck Rambo and had a daughter, Reba. They traveled singing in small churches as *The Rambos*.

Her first publishing deal was with then governor of Louisiana, Jimmy Davis, who was also a popular recording artist. She received a $3000.00 signing bonus to write for BMI (Jimmy Davis Music), which was more money than she had ever earned. Her songwriting break came when she signed a record deal with Warner Bros. Records. In 1968 she won a Grammy Award for Best Soul Gospel Performance for her album *It's The Soul Of Me.* She then signed with Benson Records and producer Phil Johnson. Her career as a songwriter and artist made her one of the legends in Christian Music.

She wrote more than 2,500 songs, including her most notable, "He Looked Beyond My Fault and Saw My Need," "We Shall Behold Him," and "Tears Will Never Stain the Streets of That City." Her songs have been recorded by a virtual "who's who" in the music world. Her biggest cut was by Whitney Houston version, "I Go To The Rock" which appeared on the motion picture soundtrack for *The Preacher's Wife*. Other secular artists who have recorded Dottie Rambo compositions, include Solomon Burke, Johnny Cash, Carol Channing, Barbara Fairchild, Larry Gatlin, Crystal Gayle, Vince Gill, Wanda Jackson, George Jones, Alison Krauss, Jerry Lee Lewis, Barbara Mandrell, Bill Monroe, The Oak Ridge Boys, Dolly Parton, Elvis Presley, Little Richard, Jeannie C. Riley, Connie Smith, Hank Snow, Mel Tillis, Rhonda Vincent, Porter Wagoner, and Dottie West.

Dottie had her own series, *Dottie Rambo Magazine*, in the 1980s on TBN. It was the No. 1 rated program on the network for six years and has rerun on and off since.

In 1987, Rambo suffered a ruptured disk which led to paralysis in her left leg. She underwent a series of surgeries that eventually reinstated limited mobility.

In 2000, Rambo was awarded the ASCAP Lifetime Achievement Award.

In 2002, Rambo reentered the studio with executive producer, Phil Johnson, to record her first solo album in eighteen years. The result was the award-winning hit "Stand By The River." The title track, a duet with Dolly Parton, went to the number one spot of the Christian Country Radio Chart, as did its follow-up, "I'm Gonna Leave Here Shoutin'."

In 2004, a major live concert DVD/CD project, *We Shall Behold Him: A Tribute to Dottie Rambo,* was released. The concert was hosted by Barbara Mandrell and included performances by Dolly Parton, Crystal Gayle, Larry Gatlin, The Isaacs, Jessy Dixon, Vestal Goodman, The Speers, The Crabb Family, and Albertina Walker.

# Celebration of Life

More than 1000 fans, friends and family members gathered at a 3-hour memorial service that was held at Christ Church on Old Hickory Blvd in Nashville, Tennessee on May 19, 2008. The 1:00 service was full hours before the service began. Both country and gospel artists filled the church to pay honor to Dottie Rambo. Among the list of Gospel singers who attended were Bill and Gloria Gaither. The Lee College Singers were on stage while groups and artists performed. Those who sang and were in attendance included Lulu Roman, The Isaacs, The Crabb Family, Andre Crouch, and Sandi Patty and more. Barbara Mandrell spoke along with Gloria Gaither. There were 17 of her songs performed by various artists that included: "Sheltered in the Arms of God," "He Looked Beyond my Fault," "I Go to the Rock," "Mamma's Teaching Angels How to Sing," "I Will Glory in the Cross," and "I've Never Been This Homesick Before."

## Final Resting Place

Woodlawn Memorial Park Cemetery
660 Thompson Lane
Nashville, TN 37204

## Bob Wills

## 1905-1975

B ob Wills died May 14, 1975 of bronchial pneumonia. He was 70.

Bob Wills was born March 6, 1905 in Limestone, Texas, the son of a champion fiddler and struggling cotton farmer. Bob's love for music was part of his life playing the fiddle for ranch dances and love for the blues and jazz. He left home at 16 and traveled from town to town. He attended barber school during his 20s and worked as a barber while still playing music. Wills formed several bands as he played radio stations around the south.

In 1934 he formed his Texas Playboys band. Bob appeared in a tailored double-breasted suit and polished custom-made boots, and the Texas Playboys dressed in business suits, white shirts, and neckties. They were on their way to becoming the largest and most famous Western band in the history of America, and their image was "Western chic."

In the 1940s expanding his band's sound with horns and a jazz-like sound. The band found national popularity into the 1940s with such hits as "Steel Guitar Rag," "New San Antonio Rose," "Smoke On The Water," "Stars And Stripes On Iwo Jima," and "New Spanish Two Step."

Wills was the composer of "San Antonio Rose" and starred in 26 movies. He was universally known as the King of Western Swing.

Wills had a heart attack in 1962 and a second one the next year, which forced him to disband the Playboys although Wills continued to perform solo.

Then in 1969 he had a stroke that left his right side paralyzed, ending his active career. However in 1973 Merle Haggard joined Bob Wills and his band for a final recording session titled *Bob Wills and His Texas Playboys: For the Last Time.*

The Country Music Hall of Fame inducted Wills in 1968 and The Rock and Roll Hall of Fame inducted Wills and the Texas Playboys in 1999.

## Celebration of Life

About 500 friends and family paid final respects Thursday to Bob Wills at Eastwood Baptist Church. Former Rep. Clem McSpadden delivered the eulogy. There were about 50 wreaths, some designed in the shape of a fiddle, surrounded Wills' closed casket. Mourners from throughout the Southwest were seated in the sanctuary two hours before the funeral.

Much of the gathering was comprised of original members of Wills' band, "The Texas Playboys."

Wills' classics including "Faded Love," "Maiden's Prayer," and "San Antonio Rose," were played by a quartet consisting of guitarist Eldon Shamblin and fiddle men, Johnny Gimble, Curley Lewis and Keith Coleman.

The coffin was removed to the church foyer and opened as mourners filed past the man who was once the nations highest paid and most sought after bandleader. Wills came home like his album said, … "For the Last Time."

# Final Resting Place

Memorial Park Cemetery
5111 So Memorial Drive
Tulsa, OK 74145

## Amanda Blake

## 1929-1989

Amanda Blake died Wednesday August 16, 1989 at 7:15 p.m. in Sacramento's Mercy General hospital where she had been a patient for three weeks after experiencing deteriorating health in a 12-year battle with throat cancer. Blake's dog, Butterfly, which she described as "a little mutt" that Blake had rescued from a pound, was also with the actress at the time of her death. She was 60.

Although she had throat cancer at the time at her death, it is widely believed that she had contracted the HIV virus from her ex-husband and had died of AIDS related complications. Blake had smoked two packs of cigarettes a day until cancer first struck in 1977 in the form of a tumor under her tongue. She had surgery and reconstruction of her mouth and taught herself to talk again. She became a supporter of the American Cancer Society and made fundraising appearances throughout the country.

Beverly Louise Neill was born on February 20, 1929 in Buffalo, New York. Blake made her stage debut at age 10 in a school pageant in her hometown.

She signed a contract with MGM while a teenager, first performing in the 1950 film, *Stars in My Crown*. Her other film credits included *Duchess of Idaho, Lili, Sabre Jet, A Star Is Born, About Mrs. Leslie* and *High Society*.

Her big success came as Kitty Russell, saloonkeeper, in the hit western *Gunsmoke*. *Gunsmoke* was TV's longest running Western as well as its longest running prime-time series with continuing characters. At 27 years old she became a household name. She left the show in 1974 after 19 years because she said she was tired. *Gunsmoke* ran from 1955-1974.

After *Gunsmoke*, Blake semi-retired while living in Phoenix, Arizona. She devoted a lot of her time working with her husband at their animal compound running an experimental breeding program for Cheetah's. They were some of the first to breed cheetah's successfully in captivity, and raised seven generations of cheetahs. A crusader for animal rights, she had been known for bringing her pet lion, Kemo, onto the *Gunsmoke* set.

## Celebration of Life

A memorial service was held in Sacramento, CA. At 10:00 a.m. Thursday morning a memorial service was held at the Sacramento Garden Chapel 6100 Stockton Blvd. Sacramento, CA

There were tears and laughter at the non-religious memorial service per her request. Caras, who with his wife, Jill, shared Blake's interest in animals and frequently traveled together, lead the service. They shared that Amanda didn't like watching herself on television. "When people around her watched her shows, she'd be under the rug or writhing in the corner. She loved going on safaris to Africa. But she insisted on taking an iron, an ironing board and bathroom scales. She'd show up on a prairie, wearing eyelashes with her nails done and clothes pressed."

A second memorial service was held on August 25th at 11:30 a.m. at Pierce Brothers Westwood Chapel 1218 Glendon Ave., Los Angeles, CA. Her friends asked that no flowers be sent to the memorial service, but instead contributions be made to the Amanda Blake

Memorial Fund in care of the Farmers and Merchants Bank of Galt, or the local animal Humane Society.

## *Final Resting Place*

Her body was cremated, and, in accord with her wishes, her ashes were scattered in the African country of Kenya, where she made many trips to view wild animals in the later years of her life.

# Bob Hope

# 1903-2003

Bob Hope died Sunday night at 9:29 p.m. on July 27, 2003 at his home in Toluca Lake of complications from pneumonia. He was 100 and surrounded by his family.

Leslie Townes Hope was born on May 29, 1903 in Eltham, London, England. His parents immigrated to the US in 1908. Hope became a US citizen in 1920. After high school he had various jobs. For two years he taught dance classes. He also boxed some under the name of Packy East, did comedy bits, sang and doubled on the saxophone.

Bob became an American comedian, vaudevillian, actor, singer, dancer, athlete and author. With a career that spanned nearly 80 years, Hope appeared in more than 70 short and feature films, including a series of "Road" movies. He was the master of one-liners.

Hope never won an Oscar for acting; he was honored four times by the Academy of Motion Picture Arts and Sciences for his contributions to the world of entertainment. He also received the Jean Hersholt Humanitarian Award in 1959. He began emceeing the Oscars in 1940, and for years hosted the televised Academy Awards.

The comedian began entertaining servicemen and women at U.S. bases in 1941—starting at California's March Field near Riverside — and in 1948 began annual Christmas shows at American bases overseas. Hope was never a member of the military. But on Oct. 29, 1997, when he was 94, he became the first American designated by Congress as an "honorary veteran of the United States Armed Forces."

When Hope turned 95, he donated his personal papers, his radio and television recordings and broadcasts, prints of movies, scripts, photographs, posters and 100,000 jokes to the Library of Congress, along with several million dollars to preserve the collection.

Hope called his success luck but then added, "The harder I work, the luckier I get."

## Celebration of Life

Bob's funeral mass was held July 29, 2003 at 6:30 a.m. Wednesday morning at St Charles Borromeo Catholic Church near Hope's estate. About 100 family members and close friends attended the secret service. Kathryn Crosby, widow of Bing Crosby attended along with Bob Gates, the pilot who flew Bob and his troupe to the Vietnam War zone. The casket was draped in an American flag which was placed in front of the altar. There were readings by his son and grandson. His other son paid tribute to his father and expressed the family's appreciation for those attending.

There was a public memorial on August 17 at the Academy of Television Arts & Sciences in North Hollywood.

# *Final Resting Place*

San Fernando Mission Cemetery
11160 Stranwood Avenue
Mission Hills, CA 91345

Police led a 25-car procession to the San Fernando Mission Cemetery,
in Mission Hills. Hope's grave is located inside a gated family garden
and Grotto. A short Scripture was read at the cemetery and then
everyone gave Hope his last standing ovation.

# 1906-1959

Lou Costello died at 3:55 pm on March 3, 1959 of a heart attack in Doctors Hospital, Beverly Hills, California. It was only three days before his 53rd birthday. He had been in the hospital for about a week after he collapsed at his apartment while watching television.

That morning around 10:30 a.m. Castello had eaten a strawberry milkshake and was feeling good. He was happy and looking forward to appearing on the *Steve Allen TV Show* on April 12. He sent his wife and former partner, Bud Abbott, home while he worked on ideas for a new routine. When Abbott heard of his passing he sobbed, saying he'd lost the best pal anyone ever had.

Louis Francis Cristill was born March 6, 1906 in Paterson, New Jersey.

Costello was an amateur boxer using a fake name so his mother wouldn't find out what he was doing. He won 32 straight fights before being knocked out. The loss, combined with the fact that his mother finally found out what he was doing, ended his boxing career.

He appeared in several silent films in the late 1920s as a stunt man before he and his partner  Bud Abbott made their debut as a comedy team in *One Night in the Tropics* (1940).

Their performance of "Who's on First?" in the film *The Naughty Nineties* (1945) became one of their most famous routines. They performed it for President Franklin D. Roosevelt and a clip plays on a video at the Baseball Hall of Fame in Cooperstown, New York.

Tragedy struck Lou and his wife in November 1943: His only son, Lou Costello Jr., drowned in the swimming pool of the family home just days before his first birthday. Lou never got over it.  That year Lou was stricken with rheumatic fever, which halted the production of any new Abbott and Costello features for over a year until Lou fully recuperated. The disease, which normally strikes children, damaged his heart and led to the heart attack that ultimately killed him at such a young age.

After highly successful career the team split up in 1957, with both winding up completely out of money after troubles with the Internal Revenue Service.

## Celebration of Life

Costello's body was taken to Steen's Mortuary, 11305 Magnolia Blvd., North Hollywood, where a rosary was recited Friday at 8 p.m.

A Requiem Mass followed Saturday at 10 a.m. at St. Francis de Sales Catholic Church, 4246 Fulton Ave., Studio City, CA.

# Final Resting Place

Calvary Cemetery
4201 Whittier Blvd
Los Angeles, CA 90023

## Larry Fine

## 1902-1975

Larry Fine died on Friday, January 24, 1975 of a stroke. He had suffered several additional strokes before his death. He was 75.

Louis Feinberg was born October 5, 1902 in Philadelphia, Pennsylvania.

Larry started playing the violin because of an accident with oxalic acid, a substance his mother used as a Jeweler. The acid burned through his skin to the muscles in his arm. He was able to get a skin graft but the muscles were weak. The doctor recommended boxing to strengthen his muscles but instead he started playing the violin. He was so talented that he played with the Philadelphia Orchestra at age nine. He also performed as a violinist in vaudeville at an early age. In 1925 he met Moe Howard and Ted Healy and they became the "three" Stooges. Larry's bushy hair became his trademark. Beginning in 1933, The Three Stooges made 206 short films, and several features. In 1934 they replace Healy, due to his drinking and abuse, with Curly Howard who shaved his head for the part. All three began to have equal shared screen time. Larry's on screen goofiness was an extension of his own relaxed personality.

Larry was described as a social butterfly off stage. He was always agreeable and was easy to work with. However he was not a good businessman spending his money as soon as he got it. Because his wife disliked housekeeping they lived in hotels. Not until the 1940s did Larry buy a home in Los Angeles.

He and his wife loved having parties and every Christmas threw lavish midnight suppers. His wife died suddenly on May 30, 1967 just a few years after The Stooges became a big hit on television.

In 1970 while the Stooges were working on a new TV series he suffered a stroke that paralyzed the left side of his body. He eventually moved into a show business retirement community in Woodland Hills. He used a wheelchair during the last five years of his life.

## *Celebration of Life*

Fine's funeral was held Monday January 27th at 2:00 p.m. at the Church of the Recessional at Forest Lawn Glendale.

## *Final Resting Place*

Forest Lawn Memorial Park Glendale
1712 South Glendale Avenue
Glendale, CA 91025

**LARRY FINE**

**1902 – 1975**

## Clark Gable

# 1901-1960

Clark Gable died at 11:00 p.m. Wednesday night November 16, 1960 at Hollywood Presbyterian Hospital. He had been hospitalized since November 6 with a heart attack. His wife had been staying in the hospital with him. They had eaten together a few hours before his death. Gable was awaiting the birth of his first child in March with current wife Kay Williams Speckles. John Clark was born at the same hospital his father died at on March 20, 1961.

It was later revealed that Loretta Young and Clark Gable had a daughter that was kept a secret.

William Clark Gable was born on February 1, 1901, in Cadiz, Ohio. It was after a high school play of *The Bird of Paradise*, that Gable decided he wanted to become an actor. When he turned 21 he left home to begin touring with a second rate stock companies. His break came in 1930 after appearing in a Los Angeles stage production of *The Last Mile*. And the rest is history.

Gable starred with many of the most popular and beautiful actresses of their time. His most famous role was Rhett Butler in *Gone With The Wind* in 1939. He earned an Oscar nomination for Best Actor and his line "Frankly, my dear, I don't give a dam" is the most famous lines in cinema. In 1934, he won an Academy Award for *It Happened One Night* and other successful films included *Mutiny on the Bounty*.

Gable was married to movie star, Carole Lombard in 1939 until her tragic death in a plane crash in 1942. The grief stricken actor put his movie career on hold for 3 years and joined the US Army Air Force.

He returned to acting and his last film was *The Misfits* released after his death in 1961 staring Marilyn Monroe.

## Celebration of Life

Clark's funeral was held on November 19 at Forest Lawn Memorial Park in Glendale, in the Church of the Recessional. The closed casket was covered in red roses with a crown made of yellow roses. The air force chaplain presided over the funeral and 200 mourners who attended with no eulogy. The air force guardsmen sounded taps.

Pallbearers were Jimmy Stewart, Spencer Tracy and Robert Taylor as well as other long time friends. The attendees included Roy Rogers, Dale Evans, Jack Benny, Ann Southern, Marion Davies, Robert Stack, Van Johnson and more.

# *Final Resting Place*

Forest Lawn Memorial Park Glendale
1712 Glendale Ave
Glendale, CA 91025

The entombment was delayed until November 23rd because of construction delays at Forest Lawn. Gable was laid to rest beside his third wife, Carole Lombard, as he requested, in The Great Mausoleum, Sanctuary of Trust. He was buried with his wedding ring, his St. Jude medal and the same navy blue suit he wore at his wedding to Kay. Only Kay and her two children were present.

## Dan Blocker

# 1928-1972

Dan Blocker died unexpectedly on May 13, 1972 following complications of a "routine" gall bladder surgery. He was 43.

Bobby Dan Davis Blocker was born December 10, 1928 in De Kalb, Texas. He weighed a whopping 14 lbs at birth. By the age of 12 he was 6' tall and weighed 200 lbs. Blocker graduated with an English degree, but fell in love with acting when he was cast in a campus production. He later got a master's degree in dramatic arts and taught school.

He moved to California to pursue a PhD at U.C.L.A. and it was reported he was seen inside a phone booth making a call dressed in his Texas standard attire (plaid shirt, jeans, boots and straw hat) and was invited to an audition. Even after he was cast in *Bonanza*, he intended to complete his PhD.

Hoss Cartwright was a gentle giant of 6'4" and 300 lbs. His role was warm and empathic and helped ground the show. He was friendly and upbeat and brought empathy to the show. His role in *Bonanza* was from September 1959 until his death in 1972.

The producers of *Bonanza* decided to write his death, by an accident, into the script. This was the first time in television history a show had dealt with one of its characters death. So as the cast mourned so did the fans although it was years later before Hoss' death was explained.

Bonanza aired from 1959–1973 with reruns going strong for over 40 years.

Dan Blocker owned a chain of restaurants called "Bonanza." They were steakhouses similar to the "Golden Corral" chain. When the ownership later changed, all of the restaurants were renamed "Ponderosa." Blocker was a millionaire many times over.

## Celebration of Life

Mrs. Blocker requested no flowers be sent to the funeral home, or later to the burial site in De Kalb, Texas, where Daniel Blocker was born. Instead, she suggested that in memory of her husband, donations be made to the Guyot Foundation Home for Girls, 721 Crenshaw Blvd., Los Angeles, California 90005.

# Final Resting Place

Woodmen Cemetery
NE Front Street
De Kalb, TX 75559

Hanner Funeral Home supervised the private burial attended by only 20 members of the immediate family. Blocker was laid to rest in the family plot between his father and his sister in a modest casket. His mother placed some roses she had picked that morning at the head of the casket.

Rev. Arthur Frey of De Kalb's First Baptist Church briefly praised Dan Blocker as a man of gentle heart and good will. Then the casket was lowered into the grave of the town's age-old Woodmen Cemetery.

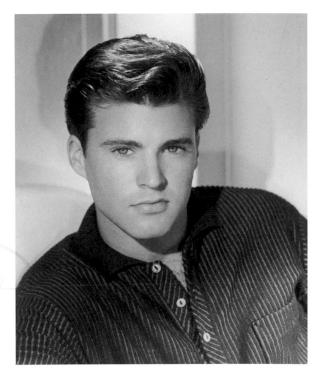

## Ricky Nelson

# 1940-1985

R icky Nelson, teen heartthrob, died in an airplane crash on December 31, 1985 in De Kalb, Texas.

It was reported that the pilot advised air traffic controllers that there was smoke in the cockpit and the DC-3 would not be able to reach the nearby airport. While attempting to land, the plane struck transmission wires, a utility pole and ran into trees. There was a fire upon impact. The pilots were the only ones to survive by escaping through the cockpit windows. Rick, his fiancée and 5 band members died.

Eric Hilliard Nelson was born May 8, 1940 in Teaneck, New Jersey. He was the second son of Ozzie and Harriet Nelson.

In 1952, Nelson was only 11 years when he was on *The Adventures of Ozzie and Harriet.* From the beginning until the end of the show's run Ricky never stopped stealing scenes. Harriet once joked, "It'll be a wonder if David doesn't murder Ricky in his bed some night."

*The Adventures of Ozzie and Harriet* TV show was actually filmed in the family's real Hollywood Hills home and the show was based on their real family.

It ran from 1952 to 1966. Ricky became one of the most popular teen idols in the late 1950s and early 1960s. His many hit songs, include "I'm Walkin'," "Travelin' Man," "Poor Little Fool," "For You," "Fools Rush In," "It's Late," "Garden Party," and "Mary Lou." Most of these songs were originally introduced on *The Adventures of Ozzie and Harriet* TV show.

After the show was canceled, Ricky Nelson devoted his time to his singing career. He was inducted into the Rock and Roll Hall of Fame in January 1987 and received a star on the Hollywood Walk of Fame on September 17, 1975.

## Celebration of Life

Nelson's remains were misdirected in transit from Texas to California, delaying the funeral for several days.

On January 6, 1986, 250 mourners entered the Church of the Hills for funeral services while 700 fans gathered outside. The service began with a 20-minute sermon before his daughter, Tracy gave the eulogy. She said of her dad "He was the kindest many you ever met. The man had class. He was an artist - He was wise – and he loved ice cream." Attendees included 'Colonel' Tom Parker, Connie Stevens, Angie Dickinson, and dozens of actors, writers, and musicians. David Nelson read condolences from President Reagan and led the congregation in the Lord's Prayer.

# Final Resting Place

Nelson had a private burial.

Forest Lawn Hollywood Hills
1218 Glendon Ave
Los Angeles, CA 90024

## Debbie Reynolds & Carrie Fisher

**1932-2017 / 1956-2017**

# Carrie Fisher 1956 - 2017

Carrie Fisher died, at the age of 60, on Tuesday, December 27 after suffering a heart attack while aboard an 11-hour flight from London to Los Angeles on Friday. She was transported to the hospital but died 4 days later.

Carrie was the daughter of Debbie Reynolds and Eddie Fisher born October 21, 1956. Following both her parents in to show business, she will forever be remembered in the 1977 block buster hit, *Star Wars* as Princess Leia starring with Harrison Ford. She was only 19. Over the years she had memorable supporting roles in movies but also published multiple books, including a memoir, "The Princess Diarist." Fisher had a battle with drug addiction and mental health. She said she smoked pot at 13, used LSD by 21 and was diagnosed as bipolar at 24. She became an outspoken advocate for mental health awareness.

# Debbie Reynolds 1932 - 2017

Reynolds died on Wednesday, December 28, 2017 of a stroke at her home only one day after her daughter's death. She was 84.

Mary Frances "Debbie" Reynolds was born on April 1, 1932, in El Paso, Texas. Debbie Reynolds went on to establish a film career as one of the most popular actresses of her time. Known for an array of musicals in the 1950s, she made a star turn in *Singin' in the Rain* (1952), in which she offered a spirited performance opposite Gene Kelly and Donald O'Connor. She had a messy divorce from Eddie Fisher, who left her for Elizabeth Taylor, which made headlines in the late 1950s.

The following decade, Reynolds won the respect of her peers with her title role in the musical *The Unsinkable Molly Brown,* for which she received an Academy Award nomination. She continued to act and sing for more than 40 more years via film, television and the stage.

## Celebration of Life

### Thursday Memorial service

Friends and family members gathered at Fisher's home on a gloomy Thursday, Jan 5 in the Hollywood Hills for an intimate memorial to mourn Debbie Reynolds and daughter, Carrie Fisher. Meryl Streep carried white flowers as she walked up the driving and sang, "Happy Days Are Here Again," with the others joining in. Her daughter, Billie Lourd, delivered eulogies. 125 friends who attended included Meg Ryan, Ellen Barkin, Ed Begley Jr. Richard Dreyfuss, Penny Marshall Gwyneth Paltrow, Tracey Ullman, Buck Henry, Candice Bergen, George Lucas, Jamie Lee Curtis and Stephen Fry. Guests dined on fried chicken, collard greens, and cornbread.

### Public Service

The family mourned in private, however there was a 90-minute public memorial service held at the Hall of Liberty at Forrest Lawn Cemetery on Saturday, March 25, 2017. It was a send off with fans and friends. Todd Fisher planned and hosted not a memorial or funeral but event with an appearance by *Star Wars* robot R2-D2. There were home videos and film clips shown starring both women. There was a tap dance to "Singing in the Rain" and a live performance by the Gay

Men's Chorus of "True Colors."   Carrie's ex-finance, Dan Aykroyd spoke. Among the 1000 attendees was Fisher's beloved dog, Gary. (It was live streamed.)

## *Final Resting Place*

Forest Lawn Hollywood Hills
6300 Forest Lawn Drive
Los Angeles, CA 90068

Debbie Reynolds and Carrie Fisher had a private joint burial at Forest Lawn Memorial Park (Hollywood Hills) Friday morning January 6, 2017.  Carrie was cremated and some of her ashes were placed in one of Carrie's favorite possessions, a Giant Prozac Pill that she bought many years ago.  Some of the ashes were placed inside her mother's coffin. Mother and Daughter were placed side by side.

## Sonny James

## 1928-2016

Sonny James died Monday, February 22, 2016 in a Nashville hospice facility. He died of natural causes. He was 87.

James Hugh Loden was born May 1, 1928 in Hackelburg, Alabama. He was singing at age four on his family's radio show in Alabama. He took part in fiddle competitions as a teenager and was an accomplished guitar player. After serving in the military, and already a local celebrity, he signed with Capital Records, taking the stage name of Sonny James. In the 50s he appeared on the *Louisiana Hayride* and the *Big D Jamboree*.

His biggest hit, "Young Love," hit the top charts in 1957. He had 23 No. 1 country hits and also had 16 straight No 1 hits from 1967 to 1971. James co-hosted the first Country Music Association Awards Show in 1967. He was inducted into the Country Music Hall of Fame in 2006. He was given a star on the Hollywood Walk of Fame in 1961.

In the 60s, he made several motion pictures, including *Second Fiddle to a Steel Guitar*, *Las Vegas Hillbillies* (with Jayne Mansfield) and *Hillbilly in a*

*Haunted House.* He produced Marie Osmond's first records, including her biggest country hit, "Paper Roses."

He was given a star on the Hollywood Walk of Fame in 1961 and retired in the mid-1980's because of vocal issues.

## Celebration of Life

A Memorial Service was held Thursday February 25, 2016, 1:30 p.m., Brentwood Hills church of Christ, Nashville, TN 37220.

In lieu of flowers donations can be made to Churches of Christ Disaster Relief, Nashville, TN.

Funeral Services were Saturday, February 27, 2016 at 1 p.m., Hackleburg, AL, Hamilton Funeral Home, Hamilton, AL 35570.

## Final Resting Place

Loden Family Plot
Cedar Tree Cemetery
Hackleburg, AL 75559

Donna Reed

# 1921-1986

**D**onna Reed died at 9:17 a.m., Tuesday, January 14, 1986 at her home in Beverly Hills, California of pancreatic cancer. She was 64. She had entered Cedars-Sinai Medical Center in December for a bleeding ulcer. The malignancy was discovered during a test for ulcers.

Donna Belle Mullenger was born January 27, 1921 on a farm outside Denison, Iowa. She moved to Los Angeles after high school. During her second year of college she was elected campus queen and asked to audition by three movie studios. She soon had a string of starring roles in films that included *Calling Dr. Gillespie, See Here, Private Hargrove, The Picture of Dorian Gray, From Here to Eternity,* to name a few.

Her career spanned more than 40 years, with performances in more than 40 films. She received numerous Emmy Award nominations and the Golden Globe Award for Best TV Star in 1963.

*The Donna Reed Show* made her a household name.

She played the wife of a doctor in a small town that dealt with family crises like measles, poor report cards, and teen-age dating. The show aired from 1958 -1966. Behind the scenes she assisted as producer and director of the show. She studied and mastered both lighting and cinematography.

In 1984 she joined the cast of *Dallas,* replacing Miss Ellie, when Barbara Bel Geddes became ill. Because she had a three-year contract she filed a $7.5 million lawsuit when Miss Bel Geddes was reinstated in the role. She settled for $1 million.

Donna Reed received a star on the Hollywood Walk of Fame on February 8, 1960.

## Final Resting Place

Westwood Village Memorial Park
1218 Glendon Ave
Los Angeles, CA 90024

## Gene Autry

# 1907-1998

THE GENE AUTRY SHOW

G ene Autry died on Friday, October 2, 1998 at his home in Studio City, California. He died two days after his 91st birthday following a long battle with cancer.

Orvon Grover "Gene" Autry was born September 29, 1907 In Tioga, Texas. Will Rogers discovered him in 1926. He was working for a local railway station and occasionally played and sang for customers. Will told him that he had enough talent to get a job on the radio. Autry quit his job and found work in the music business and was known as "Oklahoma's Yodeling Cowboy" on a Tulsa, Oklahoma radio station. He wrote a hit song "That Silver-Haired Daddy of Mine," and soon became a regular on the National Barn Dance. In the mid 30's he got married and headed to Hollywood.

He starred in movies from the 1930s to the early '60s. During World War II, he took a break from his career to enlist in the U.S. Army Air Forces, serving as a pilot from 1942 to 1945. He returned to music with his hit holiday classic "Rudolph the Red-Nosed Reindeer" which charted in 1949 and has sold more than 30 million copies.

Autry had his own television show, *The Gene Autry Show* from 1950 to 1956. He was in 95 movies during his career and was one of the most important performers in the history of country music. By singing in his cowboy movies in carried country music to a national audience.

In 1956 he stopped performing, but owned four radio stations and other investments. In 1960 he became majority owner of the Los Angeles Angels baseball team. He also was the first country music singer to get a star on the Hollywood Walk of Fame.

Gene Autry ranked for many years on the Forbes magazine list as one of the richest Americans. The town of Gene Autry, Oklahoma was named in his honor.

## Celebration of Life

Gene Autry had a private funeral.

## Final Resting Place

Forest Lawn Hollywood Hills
6300 Forest Lawn Drive
Los Angeles, CA 90068

# 1932-2011

Elizabeth Taylor died early Wednesday, March 23, 2011, of congestive heart failure at Los Angeles' Cedars-Sinai Medical Center, surrounded by her four children. She had been hospitalized for six weeks.

Taylor nearly died of pneumonia in 1990 and had both hip joint replacements in 1994 and 1995. In February 1997, she had surgery to remove a benign brain tumor. During her life she had at least 20 major surgeries. She broke her back at least five times. In 1983, she acknowledged a 35-year addition to sleeping pills and painkillers and was treated for alcohol and drug abuse spending two stays at the Betty Ford clinic.

Dame Elizabeth Rosemond was born February 27, 1932 in Hampstead, London England. She was a child actress that began acting in the 40s after her family moved to Los Angeles. Her breakthrough role was in *National Velvet* in 1944. She then became one of the most famous teenage stars. In 1951 she received critical acclaim for her performance in the drama *A Place In the Sun*. She began receiving many roles with successful performances but her most noted was in 1963 when she starred in her acclaimed *Cleopatra* and was paid a record breaking 1 million dollars. After a scandalous affair with her co-star Richard Burton, they both divorced their spouses and married ... twice. They were divorced in 1974 over Burton's excessive drinking habit after 10 years of marriage. They remarried in following year then divorced again in 1976. They made 12 movies together.

Taylor was one of the most popular actresses of Hollywood's golden age. She was also savvy in business. She was the first celebrity to create her own collection of fragrances and in 2005 founded a jewelry company. Both created more wealth than during her acting career.

## Celebration of Life

Her funeral took place the following day at the Forest Lawn Memorial Park in Glendale, California in keeping with the Jewish faith. The service was a private Jewish ceremony presided over by Rabbi Jerome Cutler. The one-hour service started late due to Elizabeth's request that her body arrive 15 minutes after the scheduled starting time. Actor Colin Farrell read poetry and her grandson played a trumpet rendition of "Amazing Grace." Approximately a dozen family members and close friends attended the funeral. Barricades were set up to block access to the funeral by the media and fans. In lieu of flowers, the family asked that contributions be made to the Elizabeth Taylor AIDS Foundation.

# Final Resting Place

Forest Lawn Memorial Park
1712 Glendale Ave
Glendale, CA 91205

Elizabeth Taylor's casket was draped in gardenias, violets and lilies of the valley.  It was placed in a crypt beneath a marble sculpture of an angel located in the cemetery's Great Mausoleum.

# 1947-2009

Farrah Fawcett died at 9:28 a.m. on Thursday June 25, 2009 at St. John's Health Center in Santa Monica, California from cancer. She was 62. Her long-time partner since the mid 80's, actor Ryan O'Neal, was with her during the night and after she received her last rites of the Catholic Church. She had recently returned to St. John's for treatment of complications from anal cancer diagnosed three years earlier.

Mary Farrah was born February 2, 1947 in Corpus Christi, Texas. She attended the University of Texas at Austin before heading to Hollywood. She was noticed by casting agents and quickly began getting parts in movies. In 1973 she married actor Lee Majors but divorced nine years later. Although O'Neal and Fawcett never married they had a son in 1985.

Farrah's famous swimsuit picture/poster was shot in early 1976. She picked out the red swimsuit and did her own hair for the photo shoot. Her hair style was given the names "Farrah Do" and "Farrah Hair" that remained in Vogue for a decade. Her poster became an iconic pin-up for millions of men.

She was cast for the successful sitcom *Charlie's Angeles* shortly afterwards playing "Jill Munroe." Fawcett left the show after one season and was replaced by Cheryl Ladd. In 1984 she received three Emmy nominations for her performance in the TV movie *The Burning Bed*. Her career appeared sporadic. She posed nude for Playboy in December 1995, which stirred controversy but also sold over 4 million copies.

Fawcett's last project was a documentary chronicling her battle with cancer called *Farrah's Story*. It aired on NBC on May 15, 2009. She ends the documentary with a commentary explaining its purpose asking, *"Why is there not more research into certain types of cancer? Why doesn't our health system embrace alternative treatments that have proved successful in other countries? I have got cancer, but I'm alive. What are you fighting for?"*

## Celebration of Life

There was a private funeral Tuesday afternoon, June 30, 2009 at the Cathedral of Our Lady of Angels in downtown Los Angeles. Her son, Redmond, who was given a three-hour release from jail to say his goodbyes attended. (Redmond had been serving a jail sentence stemming from drugs). A letter was read during the service she had written to her 24-year-old son:

*'The greatest gift of my life was to be your mother. By leaving you behind I hope you will be able to work out all your troubles and grow as a person.'*

During the one-hour Catholic service there were tributes by friends and family. Former Charlie's Angels co-star Kate Jackson was there to pay tribute along with Marla Maples, Cheryl Tiegs, Dick Van Patten, and Ernie Hudson. Alana Stewart was Farrah's best friend and was not only at the funeral but also at her bedside when she passed.

# Final Resting Place

Her dark-brown casket with an array of orange and yellow flowers was transported to Pierce Brothers Westwood Memorial Park.

Westwood Memorial Park
1218 Glendon Ave
Los Angeles, CA 90024

## George Burns

# 1896-1996

THE
*George*          *Gracie*
**BURNS** and **ALLEN**
**SHOW**

George Burns died at 10:00 a.m. on March 9, 1996 at his home in Beverly Hills, California 49 days after his 100th birthday. In December a month before his 100th birthday he was well enough to attend a Christmas party hosted by Frank Sinatra. However he caught the flu, which weakened him. Burns was famous for his raspy voice, one-liners and cigars.

Nathan Birnbaum was born on January 20, 1896 in New York, New York. He began in vaudeville as a teenager before teaming up with 18-year-old Gracie, who became his wife. They became a famous comedy team both on radio and television. *The George Burns and Gracie Allen Show* ran for nearly three decades. The famous routine ending was "Say good night, Gracie" then Gracie would respond, "Good night, Gracie." The show ended in 1959 when Gracie retired.

In 1977 Burns was in a hit film, *Oh, God* and at 80 years old, he won an Oscar for his role in *The Sunshine Boys*.

After Gracie died in 1964 George continued visiting her and upon his death he had the plaque on her crypt changed (because he wanted her to have top billing) from:

**Gracie Allen Burns- Beloved Wife and Mother (1902-1964)**

To

**Gracie Allen (1902-1964) and George Burns (1896 -1996)**

**Together Again.**

## Celebration of Life

George Burns private funeral was held March 12th at the Wee Kirk o'the Heather Church at Forest Lawn Memorial Park Cemetery, Glendale, California. There were no celebrities at his funeral. About 60 friends and family filed quietly into the chapel. Friends spoke of Burns' sheer determination to succeed in show business, a quality that helped propel his career through nine decades. Morty Jacobs, his longtime pianist played a medley of old tunes that Burns had used in his stand-up act. "Sidewalks of New York, "Love Nest," and "By the Light of the Silvery Moon."

# Final Resting Place

Forest Lawn Memorial Park
1712 S Glendale Ave
Glendale, CA 91205

Burns looked forward to his 100th birthday but he also looked
forward to death saying he would be with Gracie again in Heaven.
Their crypts are together.

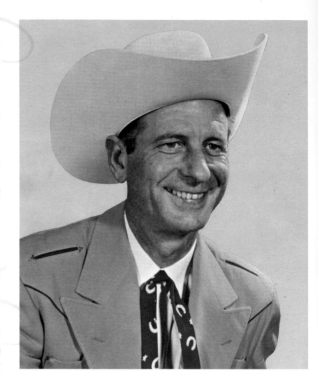

## Lloyd "Cowboy" Copas

## 1913-1963

Cowboy Copas died on March 5, 1963 in an airplane crash that also killed Patsy Cline, Randy Hughes and Hawkshaw Hawkins.

Lloyd Estel Copas was born July 15, 1913 in Blue Creek, Ohio. At 14 he started performing on radio. He moved to Knoxville and formed a band, the God Star Rangers. However it was in 1943 when Copas replaced Eddy Arnold as a vocalist in the Pee Wee King band and began performing on the Grand Ole Opry. His first solo single, "Filipino Baby," was released in 1946 and hit No. 4 on Billboard. While still performing on the Opry he released several other hits that kept his career on top during the 40s and 50s. "Signed Sealed and Delivered," "The Tennessee Waltz," "Tennessee Moon," "Breeze," "I'm Waltzing with Tears in My Eyes," "Candy Kisses," "Hangman's Boogie," and "The Strange Little Girl."

1960 was the biggest hit of his career, "Alabam," which remained number one for three months.

**The accident:** On March 3, 1963, Copas, Patsy Cline, Hawkshaw Hawkins and others performed at a benefit concert at the Soldiers and Sailors Memorial

Hall in Kansas City, Kansas. The benefit concert was for the family of disc jockey Cactus Jack Call, who had died the previous December in an automobile accident. On March 5, they left for Nashville in a Piper Comanche piloted by Copas' son-in-law (and Cline's manager), Randy Hughes. After stopping to refuel in Dyersburg, Tennessee, the craft took off at 6:07 p.m. CT. The plane flew into severe weather and crashed at 6:29 p.m. in a forest near Camden, Tennessee, 90 miles from the destination. There were no survivors.

## *Celebration of Life*

A funeral for Cowboy Copas was held on March 8, 1983 shared with his son-in-law, Randy Hughes at Phillips-Robinson Funeral Home in Nashville, Tennessee. The room was filled with flowers that had photos on each casket.

## *Final Resting Place*

Forest Lawn Memorial Gardens
1150 S Dickerson Rd.
Goodlettsville, TN 37072

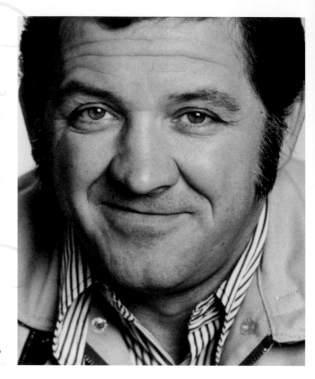

# 1928-2012

George Lindsey died on Sunday, May 6, 2012 at 12:05 a.m. after a brief illness. He was 83.

George Smith Lindsey was born in Fairfield, Alabama on December 17, 1928. Lindsey liked hanging around his Aunt Ethel's gas station as a boy, with his dogs "One Spot" and "Sappo." The mechanic hats inspired Lindsey's trademark "beanie" worn by Goober. In school he excelled in football and basketball and he enjoyed theatrical productions. His scholarships in sports allowed him to attend college where he received a degree in biological science and physical education.

After a stint in the service he landed a job as a coach and teaching history at Green High School. He said he was the worst teacher in the world and then studied theater. He signed with the William Morris Agency and began landing acting roles. After moving to California he got the call in 1962 to audition for a station attendant on *The Andy Griffith Show* but lost the part to Jim Nabors. However in 1964 he landed the role of Goober Pyle that lasted seven full seasons, four on *The Andy Griffith Show* and then three on the sequel series, *Mayberry R. F. D.* During two decades he also became a regular on the syndicated *Hee Haw.*

Lindsey became one of the busiest performers in show business. He performed in voice over work for Disney, stand-up comedy, headliner opening act and managed to record a few albums of both comedy and music.

After *Hee Haw* ended production in 1992 he continued appearing on reunion shows and hosting other shows. His last appearance in 2011 was part of the *Hee Haw* reunion, produced by Larry Black and Country's Family Reunion called *Salute to the Konfield,* created as a DVD series and TV special.

Lindsey devoted much of his spare time to raising funds for the Alabama Special Olympics. For 17 years, he sponsored a celebrity golf tournament in Montgomery, Ala., that raised money for the mentally disabled.

## Celebration of Life

Westminster Presbyterian Church, May 11, 2012 at 4:00 p.m. in Nashville, TN. Visitation was from 2-4:00 p.m. In lieu of flowers, donations in Lindsey's memory was asked to be made to Special Olympics, Alabama or another charity of choice.

## Final Resting Place

Family plot in Oak Hill Cemetery Jasper, Alabama

"I'M GLAD I MADE YOU LAUGH"

Jack Lemmon

1925-2001

Jack Lemmon died in a Los Angeles hospital on Wednesday night June 27th, although his death was not released until Thursday. His wife and children were with him when he passed away. He had been in and out of the University of Southern California/Norris Cancer Clinic in Boyle Heights Hospital as his condition deteriorated. He underwent surgery a month prior to remove an inflamed gall gladder. The cause of death was described as metastatic cancer of bladder to colon. His death came almost exactly one year after his old friend and partner in the *Odd Couple*, Water Matthau.

John Uhler Lemmon III was born February 8, 1925 in Newton, Massachusetts. He made his acting debut at four in an amateur play, but his real passion was music, and he taught himself to play piano.

Jack was a sickly boy who required 13 operations before he was 13 (some credit that experience for the quirky posture that was part of his comedic style).

He had a degree in War Services Sciences and served in the US Navy. Although his father disapproved of acting as a career, Lemmon worked in radio, theater and television.

His first movie was in 1954 with Judy Holliday in *It Should Happen To You*. He became a mainstay on TV and movies. His television show *The Odd Couple* and a stream of movies with Walter Matthau were a pleasure to watch. They were very close friends, but on the screen they were constantly at odds. Lemmon's range of talent was enormous. Of his seven Oscar nominations for lead actor, two were for comedies and five for dramas.

Lemmon co-produced the classic *Cool Hand Luke*, starring Paul Newman, and directed the 1971 film *Kotch*, which won Matthau an Oscar nomination, and composed a song for the 1957 film *Fire Down Below*, in which he starred.

Although he was well known for enjoying his martinis, he always insisted that the stories about his drinking were exaggerated. He gave up drinking, as well as smoking, at age 60.

## Celebration of Life

Lemmon's funeral was private with only friends and family invited. It was held at the Westwood Village Cemetery Chapel in Los Angeles. Some of the invited guests were Gregory Peck, Kirk Douglas, Sidney Poitier, Shirley MacLaine and Kevin Spacey.

Later there was a service held at the Paramount Studios Theater with over 500 friends and family attending. They shared stories and memories. Kevin Spacey shared the time when his dog peed on Jack's prize golf clubs. It was an evening of laughter and fun just like Jack would have wanted.

# Final Resting Place

Westwood Village Memorial Park
1218 Glendon Ave
Los Angeles, CA 90024

## Patsy Cline

# 1932-1963

Patsy Cline died on March 5, 1963 in a plane crash. She was 30.

Virginia Patterson Hensley was born on September 8, 1932, in Winchester, Virginia. As a young girl Pasty loved to dance and Shirley Temple was her idol. But as she got older she gave up her dance shoes and started singing in the church choir. As a teenager she sang on local radio stations and at dances as she worked during the day at odd jobs to help with the bills. She quit school and barely had an eight-grade education but pursued her love for music.

Patsy's first record deal was with Four Star Records in 1954. In 1955, Patsy became a regular on the radio show *Town and Country Jamboree*. However it was in 1957 when Patsy finally got her big break as a contestant on the television variety show Talent Scouts (1948), hosted by Arthur Godfrey. For her first television appearance she sang, "Walkin' After Midnight." She won first place and became a regular on the show for the next two weeks. "Walkin' After Midnight" was released as a single and put Patsy on the top ten charts of country and pop music. Patsy's trademark became her ruby red lips.

In 1960, Patsy was finally invited to join the Grand Ole Opry and the following year she scored with her second single, "I Fall to Pieces." By then she was married to Charlie Dick and had two children living in Nashville.

In March 1963, Patsy traveled from Nashville to Kansas City, to appear at a benefit concert for the family of disc jockey Jack McCall, who had been killed in a traffic accident earlier that year. Immediately after her performance, she boarded a small plane back to Nashville along with country-western performers Cowboy Copas, Hawkshaw Hawkins and pilot Randy Hughes. Approximately 85 miles west of Nashville, the plane ran into turbulence and crashed. There were no survivors.

Shortly before her death, Patsy had recorded the single "Sweet Dreams," which became #5 on the country charts after her death at age 30 her best-known song, "Crazy," was written by legend Willie Nelson).

Ten years after her death, Patsy Cline was inducted into the Country Music Hall of Fame, the first female soloist chosen for the honor.

## *Celebration of Life*

There were separate services held on Friday March 8, 1983 at Phillips-Robinson Funeral Home, Nashville Tennessee. Patsy's Casket was closed with her photo on top of her casket among the dozens of flowers.

Cline's body was then flown back to Winchester on a Tennessee National Guard airplane. Services were held on March 10 at 3:30 p.m. at Jones Funeral Home who handled all the arrangements. The chapel was packed with around 500 folks inside and hundred's more outside. To the locals it felt like a mob scene with the crowds of people lining the streets.

# *Final Resting Place*

Shenandoah Memorial Park
1270 Front Royal Pike
Winchester, VA 22602

She was buried directly after her service at Shenandoah Memorial Park in Winchester, Virginia. This was per her wishes. After the burial service a fan picked a flower from the casket. That started a frenzy of fans grabbing flowers for keepsakes.

## 1920-2000

Walter Matthau died Saturday, July 1, 2000 at 1:42 a.m. just before arriving at St John's Health Center in Los Angeles, California. The cause of death was a heart attack. He was 79. Jack Lemmon never left his side. His first heart attack was in 1965. In 1968, while filming the move *The Odd Couple,* he suffered a second heart attack. In 1975, he underwent quadruple coronary bypass surgery. In May of 1999 while in the hospital for pneumonia, they discovered colon cancer, which spread to his liver, lungs and brain.

Walter Matthow was born on October 1, 1920 in New York City, NY. On his social security card he put Foghorn as his middle name and never got around to changing it.

After high school, Walter joined the Army, and in World War II was a radioman-gunner on bombers. He actually served under Lt. Jimmy Stewart. After the service he studied acting in New York and made his Broadway debut in the 1948 *Anne of a Thousand Days.* His first movie was in 1955, in *The Kentuckian.* Matthau starred in 82 films, eight with Jack Lemmon.

# Celebration of Life

Matthau had a simple funeral on Sunday, July 2 and was buried in a plain pine casket. It was a private service with only about 50 immediate family members and a few friends.

There was a second memorial service held at the Directors Guild with invitations that specified "cheerful attire". Guests were served beer and hot dogs to capture the comedy of Matthau. Some of stars that showed up were Gregory Peck, Diane Keaton, Doris Roberts, Carl Reiner, Sophia Loren, Lauren Bacall, Jack Klugman, and Karl Malden. Larry King and Angie Dickinson. Matthau's son, film producer Charlie Matthau, was host. It included a montage of the star's work. His widow, Carol Marcus attended also.

# *Final Resting Place*

He was laid to rest on Sunday in a plain casket and simple burial,
just as he requested.

Westwood Village Memorial Park
1218 Glendon Ave
Westwood, CA  90024

Gracie Allen

# 1895-1964

THE
George          Gracie
BURNS and ALLEN
SHOW

Gracie Allen died of a heart attack on Thursday, August 27, 1964 at Cedars of Lebanon Hospital, after a long battle with heart disease. George Burns was at her side. She was 69.

Grace Ethel Cecile Rosalie Allen was born on July 26, 1895, in San Francisco, California. Her father was an entertainer and at three years old she made her stage débuted. She attended a Catholic girls' school but left at the age of 14 to join her father and sisters on stage. As a child, Allen had been scalded badly on one arm, which she was extremely sensitive about. She always wore quarter length sleeves to hide the scars. She also had one blue eye and one green eye.

She later enrolled in a secretarial school but learned a comedy team would be looking for a replacement. The new team of Burns and Allen quickly became a success. Recognizing that Allen was a natural comedian, Burns rewrote their sketches to give her the witty lines while he took a secondary role. After traveling together for three years they married on January 7, 1926, in Cleveland, Ohio.

By the 1920s, Burns and Allen were one of the most popular acts in the U.S. and were offered a contract by CBS. The switch to Radio required changes in Allen's singing and dancing. Burns suggested they play themselves, which proved a successful formula. Their show *The Burns and Allen Comedy Show* was ranked on of the top three shows in the United States. In 1937 they moved over to NBC continuing their radio show and also appearing in movies. Their move to television came in October of 1950, however after eight years Gracie retired. She was presented with a star on the Hollywood Walk of Fame and in 1988 she and Burns was inducted into the Television Hall of Fame.

*Funny Story*

*After overhearing a guilt ridden phone conversation to Jack Benny of an affair, Burns presented Gracie with an expensive centerpiece. Nothing more was said, however years later Gracie told a friend "You know, I really wish George would cheat on me again, I could use a new centerpiece."*

## Celebration of Life

Gracie's funeral was on Monday at 3:00 p.m. on August 31, 1964 at the Church of the Recessional at Forrest Lawn Memorial Park. Over 300 people overflowed the chapel including some of the biggest names in show business. Outside there were more than 100 fans that listened to the service over loudspeakers. Pall bears that carried the bronze coffin covered with orchids were Jack Benny, Edward G. Robinson, and George Jessel. Mervyn Le Roy, Dr. Rexfor Kennemer and Mike Connolly. Honorary pallbearers include Kirk Douglas and Bobby Darin.

Jack Benny delivered one of the eulogies breaking down several times saying, "She deserved this recognition because she lived in a world of laughter which was partly her own creation."

# Final Resting Place

Forest Lawn Memorial Park
1712 S. Glendale Avenue, Glendale
Los Angeles County, CA 91205

# Janet Leigh

## 1927-2004

Janet Leigh died peacefully Sunday, October 3, 2004 at her Beverly Hills home with her daughters, actresses Kelly Curtis and Jamie Lee Curtis, at her side. Leigh had suffered from vasculitis, an inflammation of the blood vessels, for over a year. She was 77.

Jeanette Helen Morrison was born July 6, 1927. She had no acting experience when her photo was presented to a studio. She was signed to a seven-year contract. Prior to her first movie in 1947, *The Romance of Rosy Ridge*, the studio changed her name. During her career she starred in about 50 movies.

In 1948 she played Meg in *Little Women* and also co-starred with Lassie in *Hills of Home*. In 1949 she played June Forsyth in *The Forsyth Saga*.

Janet took the most famous shower in history. But it was the one shower scene in the Alfred Hitchcock movie *Psycho* in 1960 that made movie history. Leigh recalls the experience as matter-of-fact. Hitchcock followed the storyboard precisely and they worked on it for about a week. It was filmed very professionally and quickly, but she did comment, "It was, of course, grueling to stand in a shower getting drenched for a week". Audiences will forever remember those fateful 45 seconds of the dying Leigh, glimpsed in naked silhouette, her hands tearing vainly at the shower curtain as her blood spirals down the drain. She earned an Oscar nomination as best supporting actress for that scene.

Her marriage to actor heartthrob, Tony Curtis in 1951 accelerated her career making several movies in the 50s together. They divorced in 1962. Her movies *Touch of Evil* and *The Manchurian Candidate* in the 60s, continued to establish her as a successful actress.

## Celebration of Life

Leigh's 17-year-old granddaughter, Annie gave an unexpected and insightful eulogy. She described seeing her grandmother after she had died and mused that she felt her death might, in fact, be her greatest accomplishment - because at that moment she was finally able to let go of the clenched control of her life; she was able to trust in her family - that she could go and we'd all be fine.

Leigh had requested that donations be made to the Motion Picture and Television Fund.

# Final Resting Place

Westwood Memorial Park
1218 Glendon Ave,
Los Angeles, CA 90024

## Floyd Cramer

# 1933-1997

Floyd Cramer died New Year's Eve, December 31, 1997 at his home in Nashville, Tennessee of lung cancer. He was 64.

Floyd Cramer was born in Sampti, Louisiana on October 27, 1933 and grew up in Huttig, Arkansas. His parents bought him a small piano when he was five and he taught himself to play. After high school he returned back to Louisiana and found work playing the piano at KWKH radio station that broadcast *The Louisiana Hayride*. He ended up backing a lot of the stars like Web Pierce, Red Sovine and Hank Williams.

In 1953 he cut his first single, "Dancin' Diane." He then toured with a new talent, Elvis Presley. Cramer played the piano on Elvis Presley's "Heartbreak Hotel." In 1957 he signed with MGM and had his first bit success as a solo act with "Flip, Flop and Bop." It was followed by "Last Date" and "On the Rebound," which topped the British pop charts. He continued to play session work as his own success flourished. He had developed his own distinctive sound described as a "bent note" or "slip note" style – hitting a note and almost instantly sliding into the next. His style influenced a generation of pianists.

His successful career continued to kept him in demand for concert tours including one of the most successful, "The Masters Festival of Music," where he co-headlined with Chet Atkins and Boots Randolph. He continued to tour up until he was diagnosed with cancer in April 1997. He had more than 50 albums to his credit.

Cramer was voted Keyboard Player of the Year by the Academy of Country Music seven times. In 2003, Floyd Cramer was inducted into both the Country Music Hall of Fame and the Rock and Roll Hall of Fame.

In the words of the late country star Jimmy Dean, "No orator ever spoke more eloquently than Floyd Cramer speaks with 88 keys."

## *Final Resting Place*

Springhill Cemetery
5110 Gallatin Rd
Nashville, TN 37216

# 1913-1989

Jim Backus died of pneumonia July 3, 1989 at St. John's Hospital and Health Center in Santa Monica, California. Backus, who had Parkinson's disease for many years, had entered the hospital more than two weeks earlier. He was 76.

James Gilmore Backus was born on February 25, 1913, in Cleveland, Ohio. He worked for a stock theater company during his teens. After high school he talked his father into letting him attend the American Academy of Dramatic Arts in New York City instead of a traditional college. Backus spent two years after graduation working in stage productions and radio. He molded his voice into different characters with his biggest radio success in 1940.

It was his acting that brought him the biggest success. Backus had appeared in about 80 films and 500 film and television episodes of *Mr. Magoo*, a near-sighted cartoon character. Backus spent three years on the sitcom *I Married Joan*, which debuted in 1951. Then came *Gillian's Island* that ran from 1964 to 1967. Backus played one of the seven castaways stranded together on an

Island. His character, Mr. Thurston Howell III was a privileged, uptight rich man stranded with his wife. He also starred in his own show for one season, *The Jim Backus Show,* also known as *Hot off the Wire.*

Backus was an avid golfer and actually made the 36-hole cut at the 1964 Bing Crosby Pro-Am Tournament. He received a star on the Hollywood Walk of Fame on February 8, 1960.

In 1978 he was reprising the role for the 1978 television movie *Rescue from Gilligan's Island* when he learned that he had Parkinson's disease. He continued acting until 1981.

## Final Resting Place

Westwood Village Memorial Park
1218 Glendon Ave
Los Angeles, CA 90024

John Wayne

1907-1979

John Wayne died at 5:23 p.m. on June 11, 1979 at U.C.L.A Medical Center of complications from cancer. He was 72.

On January 10th, Wayne entered the hospital for a routine gall bladder operation. Two days later his stomach was removed in a 9-hour operation when a cancerous tumor was discovered. Then on May 2, he was admitted for his second cancer operation. His lower intestine was partly removed in the operation.

Marion Robert Morrison was born May 26, 1907 in Winterset, Iowa. His family moved to southern California when he was a boy. He had an Airedale dog named "Duke" growing up which was Wayne's own nickname as an adult. He did well in school academically and played football well enough to receive a football scholarship to USC in 1925. He became a stuntman while exchanging football tickets for summer work. That is when he met his longtime friend, director John Ford. As he began getting bit parts in movies he changed his name to John Wayne. His first acting role was a cowboy, Breck Coleman, in the 1930 film, *The Big Trail*. He did more than 70 low budget western movies and adventures until he got his big break in 1939 with his hit *Stagecoach*. It made Wayne a star immediately.

He made over 200 films during his 50-year career with many of his movies becoming classics. He also toured the world and entertained troops for the USO.

From 1942-1943 he was in a radio series, *The Three Sheets to the Wind*.

He received the Best Actor nomination for *Sands of Iwo Jima* in 1949 and received an Oscar for his role as the one-eyed Rooster Cogburn in the classic *True Grit* in 1969. And he will always be remembered for his parts in the cavalry trilogy – *Fort Apache* (1948), *She Wore a Yellow Ribbon* (1949) and *Rio Grande* (1950).

In 1960 he produced, directed and starred in *The Alamo* along with *The Green Berets* in 1968. His began to have health issues and even had a lung removed in September 1964 (could have been the result of his six-packs-a-day cigarette habit) and in 1978 he had heart surgery to replace a valve.

Later in life, he increasingly spoke out on national issues, and played a central role in helping to get the United States Senate to ratify the Panama Canal Treaties in 1977, shortly before his death. He was awarded the Congressional Gold Medal and the Presidential Medal of Freedom. But his legacy and dying wish, was that his family and supporters use his name and likeness to help the doctors fight cancer—that led to the creation of the John Wayne Cancer Foundation (JWCF) in 1985.

Wayne's yacht, the Wild Goose, was one of his favorite possessions. He kept it docked in Newport Harbor and it was listed on the U.S. National Register of Historic Places in 2011.

## *Celebration of Life*

On Monday, June 11, 1979, the flame of the Olympic Torch at the Coliseum in Los Angeles was lit honoring John Wayne, and his memory. It remained lit until the funeral four days later, Friday, June 15, 1979. The funeral and interment was private. The family suggested, instead of flowers, donations to be sent to the John Wayne Memorial Cancer Fund at the UCLA Medical Center.

# Final Resting Place

Pacific View Memorial Park
3500 Pacific View Dr
Corona del Mar, Newport Beach, CA 92625

John Wayne's grave was left unmarked for many years because of family fears that it would be vandalized. In 1999 a plaque was placed on his grave.

It reads: "Tomorrow is the most important thing in life. Comes into us at midnight very clean. It's perfect when it arrives and it puts itself in our hands. It hopes we've learned something from yesterday.

## Merv Griffin

# 1925-2007

$M$erv Griffin died Sunday August 12, 2007 of prostate cancer. He was first diagnosed with prostate cancer in 1996, and was being treated at Cedars-Sinai Medical Center for a recurrence. He was 82.

Mervyn Edward Griffin Jr. was born July 6, 1925 in San Mateo, California. He started playing the piano at age four taking lessons from a music conservatory near his home.

He was always recruiting kids in his block as actors and audience or stage-hands. He always wanted to be the producer.

In 1945 he sang and hosted his first radio show. Griffin moved on as vocalist for Freddy Martin's band, and later as film actor and TV game and talk show host.

His show *The Merv Griffin Show* lasted more than 20 years and is what brought him the most fame. He was the producer and creator of *Jeopardy* and *Wheel of Fortune.* Griffin sold the rights to Coca Cola's Columbia Pictures Television Unit for $250 million in 1986 and retained a share of the profits. He purchased the Beverly Hilton and then acquired Resorts International in both Atlantic City and the Bahamas. He told Life magazine in 1988, "This may sound strange, but it parallels the game shows I've been involved in." Over the years, he bought and sold more than 20 hotels, gaming resorts and riverboats.

Griffin was a visionary and never stopped working, not until the very end. At the time he entered the hospital he was working on a new syndicated game show called *Merv Griffin's Crossword*.

## Celebration of Life

His funeral was held at the Church of the Good Shepherd on August 17, 2007 in Beverly Hills, California. Among the mourners were former first lady Nancy Regan, Pat, Sajak, Vanna White, Alex Trebeck, Dick Van Dyke, Maria Shriver and her husband, Arnold Schwarzenegger giving one of the eulogies.

## Final Resting Place

Westwood Village Memorial Park
1218 Glendon Ave
Los Angeles, CA 90024

Toto

# 1933-1945

Toto died in 1945 at the age of 13, which is 91 in human years.

Toto's real name was Terry and she was a female Terrier. She appeared in 16 different movies but the most famous was with Judy Garland in *The Wizard of Oz* filmed in 1939. She was paid $125 a week which was more than the Munkins were paid.

Interestingly she was not only a female dog billed as a male, but her name was billed wrong in the credits. After the movie became so popular her name was officially changed to Toto (but she never had a sex change).

Toto wasn't too fond of being in the basket during the filming. She suffered a sprained foot after being stepped on by one of the Wicked Witch's guards. But she finished the film with no problem and it healed nicely.

The owner and trainer was Carl Spitze. He acquired her when she was left for training and never picked up by the owners. She was a year old at the time.

# Final Resting Place

Toto was buried in the pet burial area behind Carl Spitz's residence and kennel.

In 2011 a memorial at the Hollywood Forever Cemetery, funded by an active group of Toto fans, was unveiled in memory of Toto. She is at the same cemetery as Judy Garland.

This monument is dedicated to the memory of the beloved Toto from the 1939 film, "The Wizard Of Oz." After the death of Toto, originally named Terry, in 1945, Owner and Trainer Carl Spitz buried the Cairn Terrier on his ranch in Studio City. The 1958 construction of the Ventura Freeway destroyed her resting place.

# Mickey Rooney

# 1920-2014

Mickey Rooney died on Sunday, April 6, 2014 in Los Angeles of a heart attack. He was 93. The actor began having difficulty breathing during and afternoon nap. He had passed a physical, which was required before movie appearances. He had just filmed a scene for the upcoming installment of the *Night at the Museum* with Ben Stiller .

His sole estate was valued at $18,000 after a career of more than 80 years and eight wives. His will disinherited all of his children and stepchildren, except his stepson, Mark Rooney whom he lived with.

Joseph Yule Jr was born on September 23, 1920, in Brooklyn, New York but shortly moved with his parents to Hollywood. At 10, he was already a star, appearing in shorts based on the popular *Mickey McGuire* strip.

It was the Andy Hardy film series produced between the 1930s and 1940s that made him the highest paid actor in Hollywood. He became even more popular when he was paired up with Judy Garland for three movies. In 1956 he received an Oscar nomination for *The Bold and the Brave*. Over his career he earned four Oscar nominations.

Rooney was known as a spendthrift and loved gaming on horse racing even when he didn't have much earnings.

## Celebration of Life

(There were two separate family funerals at Hollywood Forever).

One set of family members and friends held a memorial service Friday, April 18th.  A private funeral, organized by another set of family members was held Saturday, April 19th.

## Final Resting Place

Hollywood Forever Cemetery
6000 Santa Monica Blvd
Los Angeles, CA 90038

There was a court hearing as to where the actor's body would be laid to rest by his family.  Mickey Rooney's final wish was granted after his attorney fought for his final wishes.  He commented "Mickey had enough lawsuits in his life for 10 people; the last thing he needs is one over where he'll be buried."  He was laid to rest next to Hollywood legends at Hollywood Forever Cemetery.

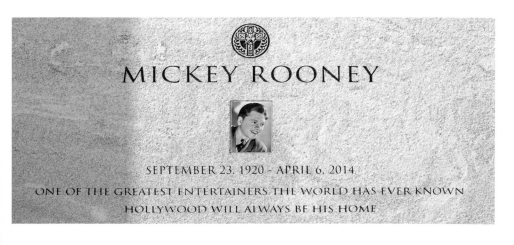

MICKEY ROONEY

SEPTEMBER 23, 1920 - APRIL 6, 2014

ONE OF THE GREATEST ENTERTAINERS THE WORLD HAS EVER KNOWN
HOLLYWOOD WILL ALWAYS BE HIS HOME

THE **LONE RANGER**

Clayton Moore died on Wednesday, December 28, 1999 in the emergency room of a hospital in West Hills, California of an apparent heart attack. He was 85.

Jack Carlson Moore was born September 14, 1914 in Chicago, IL.

Moore learned acrobatics, tumbling and swimming as a teenager. One of his instructors was Johnny Weissmuller, the champion swimmer who later played Tarzan in movies. He performed in a circus as a trapeze act for several years until an injury ended his circus career.

He then started appearing in bit parts and performing stunts in TV serials.

Moore became one of the biggest names in Western adventure as the *Lone Ranger.* His ½ hour successful TV series began Sept. 15, 1949. He played the part from 1949-1952 and 1954-1957. His theme song was the "William Tell Overture," and he rode a magnificent white steed named Silver. Each show began with the announcer describing "A fiery horse with the speed of light, a cloud of dust and hearty 'Hi Yo Silver!'"

With his faithful Indian companion, Tonto, by his side he fought for law and order. Although he packed two six-shooters, it was said he never killed anyone throughout the series.

After the TV show Moore continued the character appearing in costume. The owner's served him with a restraining order in 1979. However it was lifted in 1985 and he told a reporter, "I'll wear the white hat the rest of my life. The Lone Ranger is a great character, a great American. Playing him made me a better person."

He had a brief break while he served three years in the Army Air Force and ended up appearing in 70 feature films during his career.

Moore left behind three masks when he died. Each one dated back to the 1950s. One is in the Smithsonian, another belongs to a private collector, and third mask, which was owned by his daughter, was auctioned off for his 100th birthday.

## Celebration of Life

His funeral was private.

## Final Resting Place

Forest Lawn Memorial Park
1712 S. Glendale Ave
Glendale, CA 91205

# 1926-1962

Marilyn Monroe died on Sunday, August 5, 1962 from an overdose of sleeping pills at her home in Brentwood, California. She was 36.

Norma Jean Mortenson was born on June 1, 1926, in Los Angeles, California. Her mother was emotionally unstable so Norma Jean was reared by foster parents and in an orphanage. At 16, she married a fellow worker in an aircraft factory, but they divorced a few years later. In 1944 she did some modeling and in 1946 she changed her name to Marilyn Monroe. After signing a short-term contract with 20th Century Fox, she had a few bit parts and then returned to modeling. In 1949 she posed nude for a calendar and the next year she returned to acting appearing in minor roles. By 1950s she won international fame as the voluptuous blonde bombshell in *Gentlemen Prefer Blondes, How to Marry a Millionaire* and *The Seven Year Itch.* Her classic pose was when her white skirt billowed up by the wind from a passing train while standing over a subway grate.

In 1954 she married baseball great Joe DiMaggio but was only married eight months. She then married playwright, Arthur Miller in 1956, but divorced one week before the film *The Misfits*, which Miller had written, was released.

# Celebration of Life

Her funeral was on August 9th at the Westwood Memorial Chapel. Family and close friends made up the 31 mourners at the intimate service. Hundreds of movie fans and press lined the outside walls and on rooftops with hundreds of city police there to handle the crowd. Monroe lay in an open bronze casket wearing a simple green sheath dress and green scarf around her neck. In her hand was a tiny bouquet of baby pink roses placed there by her former husband Joe DiMaggio. It was reported he leaned over and kissed Marilyn's lips repeating, "I love you, I love you" before her casket was placed inside her crypt.

# Final Resting Place

Westwood Village Memorial Park
1218 Glendon Ave
Los Angeles, CA 90024

When Marilyn died, Joe DiMaggio was responsible for Monroe's arrangements. He chose Westwood not because of its celebrities but because it was the resting place of Monroe's mother's friend, Grace Goddard, and Goddard's aunt, Ana Lower, both of who had cared for Monroe as a child. For years after her death DiMaggio had roses sent to Monroe's crypt three times a week.

## Mel Blanc

## 1908-1989

M el Blanc died on Monday afternoon July 11, 1989 at 2:30 p.m. Mel had been hospitalized at Cedars-Sinai Medical Center since May 19, suffering a heart attack and other related problems. He was 81.

Blanc started smoking at age nine and continued his pack-a-day habit until he was diagnosed with emphysema in 1977. It was a bad cough that led to the discovery of his declining health.

Melvin Jerome Blanc was born May 30, 1908, in San Francisco, California. However the family soon moved to Oregon where he was raised. As a child he displayed his one-of-a-kind vocal gift while developing his piercing laugh into Woody Woodpecker's signature call.

In 1933 him and his wife began hosting a daily one-hour radio show in Portland called *Cobwebs and Nuts*. Because the management refused to hire additional actors, Blanc invented an entire repertory company of voices. It was only a couple of years later they moved to Los Angeles and Warner Brothers hired him. In time, Blanc provided the voices for more than 90% of Warner's stable of cartoon characters. For most of them, he helped develop the distinctive personalities.

Mel was known as "The Man of 1000 voices." He was never seen on the silver screen but his voice was known by children everywhere for over 50 years. He was the voice of Porky Pig, Bugs Bunny, Barney Rubble, Daffy Duck and countless other animated cartoon characters.

"Eh . . . what's up, Doc?" by Bugs Bunny; "I tawt I taw a putty tat," by Twitty bird; "SSSSSsssuffering SSSSSuccotash," by Sylvester. His characters were a real part of his personality. After 21 days, finally awoke, picked himself up and went back to work.

In 1961 Blanc had an automobile accident. While he was in a coma for 21 days, the doctors could not get him to respond, so one afternoon one of the doctors came in and said, *'Hey, Bugs Bunny! How are you?"* Blanc answered back in Bugs' voice. *"Ehh, just fine, Doc. how are you?"* Then the doctor aid, *"Hey Porky Pig! How are you feeling?"* And he said, *"J-j-j-just fine, th-th-th-thanks."* Blanc finally awoke, picked himself up and went back to work.

According to Blanc, Sylvester the Cat was the easiest character to voice because, "It's just my normal speaking voice with a spray at the end." Yosemite Sam was the hardest because of his loudness and raspiness.

In 1975 Blanc had diversified, forming his own production company, along with his son Noel. Noel had studied all of the character voices his father had created since he was a boy. The firm they owned together produced commercials for such products as Kool Aid, Raid and Chrysler cars and for non-profit agencies including the American Cancer Society. And in 1988, Blanc performed a bit part as Daffy Duck in the wildly successful film feature, *Who Framed Roger Rabbit?*

Over the years, Blanc received a slew of awards. In 1984 he was honored by the Smithsonian Institution.

# Celebration of Life

Warner Brothers held a memorial in Hollywood showcasing his special character friends. A print was done as a tribute.

# *Final Resting Place*

Hollywood Forever Cemetery
6000 Santa Monica Blvd
Los Angeles, CA 90038

"THAT'S ALL FOLKS"

# 1938-1981

Natalie Wood died Sunday, November 29, 1981 at 43, by drowning off Santa Catalina Island. It was reported she was attempting to board a dinghy from the family yacht, Splendour. She apparently fell hitting her face while she was getting into the boat's dinghy after an argument and landed in the water. The reports said she was wearing a goose down jacket absorbing over 40 pounds of water that possibly weighted her down to the point that she could not pull herself up. Sometime after midnight Robert Wagner discovered his wife missing along with the dinghy. They found her body the next morning floating the Pacific. The dinghy was found lodged in a cove near Catalina Island.

Natasha Gurdin was born on July20, 1938 in San Francisco, California. She was 4 years old when she appeared as an extra in her first movie, Happy Land, with her mother. It was after her family moved to Los Angeles and that she decided to change her name to Natalie Wood.

During her career she appeared in over 56 movies but her most famous role was in the Christmas classic *Miracle on 34th Street*. She made 30 movies before the age of 18. She received an Academy Award nomination for best supporting actress at 17 for *Rebel Without a Cause* opposite James Dean. On her 18th birthday she went on a studio-arranged date with then 26-year-old Robert Wagner. They made several movies together and married a year later on December 28, 1957 but divorced in 1962. They then remarried July 16, 1972 and had a daughter together in 1974.

Natalie stared in one hit after another both in film and television receiving awards for her performances. She received a Star on the Hollywood Walk of Fame on February 1, 1987.

## Final Resting Place

Pierce Bros Westwood Village Memorial Park
1218 Glendon Ave
Los Angeles, CA 90024

About 100 people gathered to say goodbye to Natalie Wood. Her husband, actor Robert Wagner sobbed as he kissed the white flowered-covered casket. The graveside ceremony included eulogies by actress Hope Lange, author Thomas Thompson and actor Roddy McCowell.

Honorary pallbearers included Laurence Olivier, Fred Astaire, Gene Kelly, Gregory Peck and Frank Sinatra who dropped flowers on the casket. Robert Wagoner plucked flowers from the casket and distributed them to her daughters.

# Stan Laurel

# 1890-1965

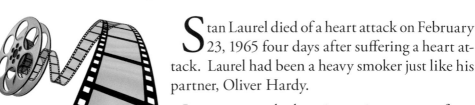

 S tan Laurel died of a heart attack on February 23, 1965 four days after suffering a heart attack. Laurel had been a heavy smoker just like his partner, Oliver Hardy.

It was reported, that just minutes away from death, Laurel told his nurse that he would not mind going skiing at that very moment. Surprised she replied that she wasn't aware he was a skier. "I'm not," said Laurel, "I'd rather be doing that than this!" A few minutes later he was dead.

Arthur Stanley Jefferson was born June 16 1890, at his grandparents house in Lancashire, England. His parents were both active in the theater. He moved to Glasgow, Scotland and finished his education. At 16 performed pantomime and music hall sketches. In 1910 he joined a troupe of actors where he became an understudy for Charlie Chaplin.

Chaplin and Laurel arrive in the US and toured with the same troupe. He teamed up with Oliver Hardy in the silent film *The Lucky Dog* in 1921. By 1924, Laurel had given up the stage for full-time film work. He worked on 12 two-reel comedies before signing with Hal Roach studios. In 1927 Laurel and Hardy started sharing the screen together and became good friends.

The fans loved their chemistry. In 1941, Laurel and Hardy signed a five-year contract with 20th Century Fox. They toured England and became even more successful. However illnesses began to plaque both actors.

Hardy had a heart attack in 1954 and died in 1957. Laurel was too ill to attend his funeral and said, "Babe would understand." (Babe was what Laurel called Hardy)

Laurel and Hardy are featured on the cover of the Beatles' album *Sgt. Pepper's Lonely Heart's Club Band* (1967).

## Celebration of Life

Dick Van Dyke gave the eulogy. He read "The Clown's Prayer." Buster Keaton was one of the stars that attended Laurel funeral and was overhead saying "Chaplin wasn't the funniest, I wasn't the funniest, this man was the funniest."

# Final Resting Place

Forest Lawn Hollywood Hills
6300 Forest Lawn Drive
Los Angeles, CA 90068

## Patty Duke

## 1946-2016

Patty Duke died Tuesday morning March 29, 2016, at 1:20 a.m. She was 69. Her cause of death was sepsis from a ruptured intestine.

Anna "Patty Duke" Pearce was born December 14, 1946 in Queens, New York. Duke became a teenage star in 1959 when she played Helen Keller in *The Miracle Worker* on Broadway with Anne Bancroft. The two-year run led to her playing the same part in the 1962 movie for which she won an Oscar and Golden Globe award. She was then given her own show, *The Patty Duke Show* ran for three years, 1963-1966 in which it earned an Emmy nomination. She played dual roles as twin cousins living in New York. In 1967, she starred in *Valley of the Dolls*, followed by *Me, Natalie*, an independent film that netted her a second Golden Globe award. Duke starred as a pregnant teenager in a made-for-TV movie, *My Sweet Charlie*. (She also won Emmys in 1977 and 1980.)

After her first divorce at 23, she started dating 17-year-old Desi Arnaz Jr, son of Lucille Ball. The scandal that was created by Lucy's disapproval ended when she suddenly married her second husband, Michael Tell. They split 13 days later and the marriage annulled. She soon started dating actor, John Astin. Her son was born in 1971.

*The Lord of the Rings* star, Sean Astin, didn't learn that he was actually adopted by Astin until he was much older. His mother told him that actor and musician Desi Arnaz Jr. was his biological father, but a paternity test later revealed that, in fact, music promoter Michael Tell was his father. Sean said in 2004 he still has relationships with all three men - the man who raised him, the man his mother claimed was his father and his actual biological father.

Although her career was very successful she struggled personally. In 1982 she was diagnosed with bipolar disorder. She became an advocate for mental health, while continuing her acting.

Duke was married four times, including a 13-year marriage to actor John Astin, best known for his role on *The Addams Family*.

## Celebration of Life

Hundreds of friends and family members attended her funeral on Saturday morning at the Lake City Church. Celebrity and long time friend, Melissa Gilbert spoke.

## Final Resting Place

Forest Cemetery
1001 N Government Way
Coeur d'Alene, ID 83814

# 1901-1966

Walt Disney died at 9:35 a.m. on December 16, 1966 in St. Joseph's Hospital in Los Angeles, California of a heart attack. His death was attributed to acute circulatory collapse. He had undergone surgery at the hospital a month earlier for the removal of a lung tumor that was discovered after he entered the hospital for treatment of an old neck injury received in a polo match. On Nov. 30 he re-entered the hospital for a "post-operative checkup." He was 65.

Walt Disney was born in Chicago, Illinois on Dec. 5, 1901. His family moved to Marceline, Mo., when he was a child and he spent most of his boyhood on a farm. When his family moved back to Chicago, he went to high school and studied cartoon drawing at night at the Academy of Fine Arts. He did illustrations for the school paper. Walt Disney never graduated from high school but he received honorary degrees including Yale and Harvard. By the end of his career he had a list of 700 awards and honors.

Mr. Disney held no formal title at Walt Disney Productions; he was in direct charge of the company and was deeply involved in all its operations. It was his incredible imagination and industrious factory of drawing boards that created the most popular movie stars ever to come from Hollywood and created one of the most fantastic entertainment empires in history. He received 29 Oscars.

He took a small garage-studio and made it into one of the most modern movie studios in the world, with four sound stages on 51 acres. He also created the nation's greatest tourist attractions, Disneyland, a 300-acre track of amusement rides.

He did none of the drawings of his most famous cartoons. Mickey Mouse, for instance, was drawn by Ubbe Iwerks, who was with Mr. Disney almost from the beginning. Iweks said Disney could have done the drawing if he wasn't so busy. However, Disney was the voice of Mickey.

He had to pawn and sell almost everything because exhibitors looked at Mickey as another cartoon. The public saw it as something a lot more. It became the most beloved of all of the Hollywood stars. But Mickey Mouse was not enough for Mr. Disney. He created Donald Duck, Pluto and Goofy. He dug into books for Dumbo, Bambi, Peter Pan, The Three Little Pigs, Ferdinand the Bull, Cinderella, Sleeping Beauty, Brer Rabbit, Pinocchio. In *Fantasia,* he added cartoon stories with classical music.

## *Celebration of Life*

There was a private family ceremony. He asked for no fan fair and was placed in the private family garden after the ceremony.

# *Final Resting Place*

Forest Lawn Memorial Park
1712 S Glendale Ave
Glendale, CA 91025

## 1894-1974

Walter Brennan died Saturday at 4:30 p.m. on September 21, 1974 at St. John's Hospital in Oxnard, California. He fought a long battle with emphysema. He had entered the hospital on July 25, his 80th birthday. Over the next few weeks his condition got steadily worse. The last years of his retirement were spent on his 12-acre ranch in Ventura County, California.

Walter Andrew Brennan was born July 25, 1894 in Lynn, Massachusetts. He studied engineering at a college in Cambridge, Massachusetts and had a variety of jobs. He acted in some school plays before touring in small musical comedy companies. He was in the military in 1917 and after the service he went to Guatemala and raised pineapples. When finally ended up in Los Angeles he speculated in real estate. In 1923 he got work as a stuntman and eventually was given speaking roles.

In 1936 he won his very first Best Supporting Actor Academy Award for *Come and Get It*. He won the award again in 1938 and 1940.

He had a wide range of acting playing sophisticated businessmen, con artists, cowhands, military men and local yokels easily. In 1932 he lost most of his teeth in an accident and started playing older roles but his career never waivered. Brennan starred in three TV series, *Tycoon*. *The Guns of Will Sonnet*, and in 1952 he played his most famous role in the TV series *The Real McCoy's* which ran for six seasons.

Brennan also recorded several albums. "Old Rivers", which first charted on April 7, 1962, spent 11 weeks on the charts, and peaking at number five. Brennan and Katharine Hepburn were the only actors to win three Oscars on 3 consecutive nominations. Brennan made more than 100 movies.

Although Brennan played "old southern, kinda hillybilly with thick southern accents, in reality he had a New England accent.

## Final Resting Place

San Fernando Mission Cemetery
11160 Stranwood Ave
Mission Hills, CA 91345

# 1897-1975

Moe Howard died Sunday night, May 4, 1975, of lung cancer at Cedars- Sinai Medical Center in Los Angeles. He had been admitted a week earlier in April just over three months after Larry Fine's death. Moe was a heavy smoker and was 77 years old.

Moses Harry Horwitz was born on June 19, 1897 in Brooklyn, New York. He was a good student in school, with an excellent memory. As a child his mother refused to cut his hair, so he finally got a pair or scissors and cut it himself revealing the bowl cut that became his trademark. Moe got the acting bug early and dropped out of high school. He joined a vaudeville act. By 1923, he and his older brother Shemp formed a Two Stooges act, and in 1925 they added Larry Fine as the third stooge. There were a few other Stooge changes but the success never altered.

Moe was the leader and known for bopping the others on the head with mallets, tweaking their noses, gouging their eyes, kicking their shins and other playful antics that never seemed to harm them. Their more than 200 18-minute comedy reels were used to fill in movie bills to a given length.

In the latter years Moe Howard and Larry Fine often teamed up together to perform at benefits in the Hollywood area. They also recorded 41 live wrap-around segments for *The New Three Stooges* cartoon series.

The Three Stooges popularity, even after the last remaining original Stooge died, are more celebrated today then they were in their career from the 1930s to the early 1970s.

## Celebration of Life

His funeral was held at 2 p.m. on May 6th at Hillside Memorial Chapel.

## Final Resting Place

Hillside Memorial Park – Culver City
6001 W Centinela Ave
Los Angeles, CA 90045

## Merle Haggard

## 1937-2016

Merle Haggard died on the morning of April 6, 2016, his 79th birthday. He died of complications from pneumonia at his home in Palo Cedro, California. He battled numerous bouts of pneumonia, and was hospitalized for 11 days earlier in the year.

Merle Ronald Haggard was born April 6, 1937. His father died when he was nine and he struggled as a young boy. His brother gave him a used guitar when he was 12 years old and it was his music that he turned to after his stay in prison and a crime he received a full and unconditional pardon for. His music was about the working class people and every day struggles. His 1967 song "Sing Me Back Home," was based on his time in solitary confinement.

Haggard's musical style came from a new wave of raw emotional music called "The Bakersfield Sound." It was not the polished, rehearsed music that had been coming out of Nashville. His good friend Buck Owens was an important part of the successful sound coming out of Bakersfield. Haggard had a string of successful songs as his popularity grew. Starting in 1966, Haggard scored 37 top 10 country hits in a row, 23 of them reaching No. 1. He was inducted into the Country Music Hall of Fame in 1994.

Merle Haggard was known by his fans as "Hag." His personal connection with his fans was as real as his life struggles. He was a masterful guitarist, fiddler, songwriter, singer and a true American success story.

## Celebration of Life

On April 9, 2016 there was a private outdoor funeral service at his ranch in Shasta County, California pre-planned by Haggard. Longtime friend and country music singer, Marty Stuart officiated and also sang "Silver Wings." Haggard had a pre-arranged sound track for the afternoon service beginning with Lefty Frizzell's recording of "I Love You a Thousand Ways." There were performances by Kris Kristofferson, Connie Smith and Ronnie Reno. The service ended with "Today I Started Loving You Again" by his three sons – Marty, Noel and Ben.

## Final Resting Place

Haggard had a private burial at Haggard Family Ranch Cemetery Palo Cedro, Shata County, California. Erich Church sent this to his fans in honor of Merle.

*"Pledge of Allegiance to the Hag"*
*Rest In Peace.*
*One of these days when my time has come*
*You can take me back to where I'm from*
*Put me on a westbound train*
*And ship me off in the pourin' rain*
*Don't cry for me when I'm gone*
*Just put a quarter in the jukebox and sing me back home and*
*Tip your hats and raise your glasses of cold cold beer*
*They say country's fading*
*But just keep waving that flag around here*
*And I know it'll keep on coming back*
*As long as people pledge allegiance*
*Where folks still pledge allegiance*
*I pledge allegiance to the Hag*

Liberace died on February 4, 1987 at 2:05 p.m. at his home in Palm Springs, California from disputed claims of validity of the cause of death. Some believe it was from complications with Aids it was reported he had been diagnosed with Aids in August 1985. He didn't seek any medical treatment for his condition and his illness was a secret until the day he died. He was given his last rites of the Catholic Church and died at age 67.

Wladziu Valentino Liberace was born on May 15, 1919 in West Allis, Wisconsin. He had a twin, who died at birth, and three other siblings. Liberace started playing the piano when he was four. His father played the French horn and had a love for music. Although his parents struggled financially, his father took him to concerts and demanded high standards of study. He had a speech impediment as a teen and his lack of interest in sports and fondness for the piano and cooking only increased his childhood teasing.

By ten years old Liberace was playing in theaters, on local radio and playing for weddings and special events. Although he adopted the stage name, Liberace, he was known to his friends as "Lee" and "Walter" to his family. His career breakthrough came in 1951 with the premier of *The Liberace Show*. It first aired in Los Angeles before going nationally after a few years. Liberace became world known as a famous as a pianist, singer, actor, and entertainer. During the 1950s-1970s he was the highest-paid entertainer in the world with a lifestyle of flamboyant excess both on and off the stage.

When Liberace died, it was reported that he was worth $115 million. He signed a will 11 days before he died leaving the bulk of his estate to the Liberace Foundation for the Performing Arts, which provides scholarships in the arts at 22 colleges and universities across the country. Some of the estate also went to his sister, Angie; a sister-in-law, Dora; a housekeeper and some friends.

His Las Vegas mansion was sold to a British businessman and fan in 2013. He received a star on the Hollywood Walk of Fame in 1988.

## Celebration of Life

About 250 family members, friends and fans attended a memorial Mass for the flamboyant pianist in Palm Springs on Friday February 6, 1987 at Our Lady of Solitude Roman Catholic Church. Those attending included actors Kirk Douglas, Isabel Sanford and Charlene Tilton. Bob Hope's wife, Delores, attended.

President Reagan sent a telegram, remembering Liberace – who used furs, jewels and a candelabra as props while performing – as "the ultimate entertainer."

## Final Resting Place

Forest Lawn Hollywood Hills
6300 Forest Lawn Dr
Los Angeles, CA 90068

FRANCES
OUR BELOVED "MOM"
1891 – 1980

LIBERACE
SON AND BROTHER
1919 – 1987

GEORGE
SON, BROTHER, HUSBAND OF DORA
1911 – 1983

"SHELTERED LOVE"

# 1915-1987

Lorne Greene died on September 11, 1987 at age 72 of complications from pneumonia after ulcer surgery, in Santa Monica, California.

Lyon Himan Green was born on Feb. 12, 1915 in Ottawa, Ontario. He was called "Chaim" by his mother. It is not known when he started using Lorne or when he changed his last name to Greene. He attended Queen's University in Kingston and became interested in broadcasting. He joined Royal Canadian Air Force during World War II and served as a Flying officer. He was assigned as a newsreader on the CBC National News. The CBC gave him the nickname "The Voice of Canada"; however because he delivered distressing war news in his deep, resonant voice and read the dreaded list of soldiers killed in the war, many listeners called him "The Voice of Doom." He also invented a stopwatch that ran backwards so announcers could gauge how much time was left, while speaking.

His TV role in *Bonanza* as the patriarch Ben "Pa" Cartwright came in 1959. He capitalized on his image in 1960 by recording several albums of western/folk songs, which was mixed with spoken words and singing. In 1954 he had a #1 single with his ballad "Ringo." When *Bonanza* was canceled in 1973 after

14 years, Greene continued to act in whatever roles he could, appearing in *Battlestar Galactic, Roots, Griff, Last of the West, Highway to Heaven, Code Red* and more.

## Celebration of Life

About 500 friends and family attended funeral services on Monday, September 15, 1987 in Culver City at Hillside Memorial Park chapel. Michael Landon and Pernell Roberts, who played two of Cartwright's three sons on *Bonanza* attended the service, Dan Blocker, who played the third son, Hoss, died in 1974. The chapel, which only seated 300, was full with the remaining 200 people seated outside. They were able to listen to the 75-minute-service over speakers set up out side.

## Final Resting Place

Hillside Memorial Park Cemetery
6001 W. Centinela Ave
Culver City, CA 90045

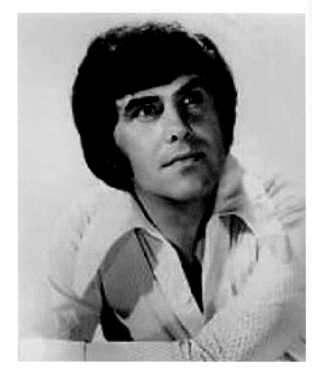

Mel Street died October 21, 1978 of a self-inflected gunshot wound on his 45th birthday at his Hendersonville home. He had just finished eating breakfast with his wife and family members, then walked up stairs and placed a .38-caliber revolver to his mouth and pulled the trigger. He had been diagnosed with clinical depression and alcoholism.

King Malachi Street was born October 21, 1935 in Rowe, Virginia. When he was 16 he performed on a live radio show for the first time. He worked as a radio tower electrician while living in Ohio but moved back to West Virginia in 1963 and opened up an auto body shop. He worked during the day and performed at night. From 1968-1972 he hosted his own television show on a Virginia station, called *Country Showcase*.

In 1970 he went to Nashville and recorded his first single, "Borrowed Angel." It took two years before it was released and became a top 10 Billboard hit in 1972. After moving to Nashville he followed up with 22 more hit songs. He then recorded his smash hit "Lovin' on Back Streets" that peaked at #5 on the US charts.

Although he was performing on national television as his career flourished with hits like "Forbidden Angel," "I Met a Friend of Yours Today," "If I Had a Cheatin' Heart," and "Smokey Mountain Memories," and " You Make Me Feel More Like A Man," he began suffering from mental health issues.

## Celebration of Life

Mel Street's funeral was at Woodlawn Chapel on October 24, 1978. Among the country stars that attended was George Jones. Jones sang "Amazing Grace" during the service.

## Final Resting Place

Woodlawn Memorial Cemetery
660 Thompson Lane
Nashville, TN 37204

## Michael Landon

# 1936-1991

Michael Landon died Monday, July 1, 1991 at the age of 54 at his Malibu ranch. He announced that he was diagnosed with pancreatic cancer on April 8, which metastasized into his liver and lymph nodes. He passed away three months later with his wife at his side.

Eurgen Maurice Orowitz was born on Saturday, October 31, 1936, in Forest Hills, Queens, New York. His athletic skills earned him a college scholarship to USC. An accident that injured his arm ended his athletic career and his term at USC. He worked odd jobs and small rolls before deciding to make a career in acting. He changed his name to a name he found in the telephone directory.

Landon made his movie debut in 1957 in *I Was a Teen-Age Werewolf*, now a cult classic. In 1959 he was cast as the romantic, spontaneous Little Jo Cartwright in *Bonanza* which ran for 14 years. It was followed by two other series, *Little House On The Prairie* and *Heaven Can Wait*.

# Celebration of Life

Michael was cremated the day after his death and his ashes were interred at Hillside Memorial Garden where the remains of Lorne Greene are located. The funeral services were private and heavily guarded only allowing those on the guest list admitted.

Former US President Ronald Regan and his wife, Nancy Reagan, attended Landon's memorial service along with former *Little House On The Prairie* cast members, Melisa Gilbert and Merlin Olsen. He was praised for his honesty and wit and loved by so many.

# Final Resting Place

Hillside Memorial Park
6001 W. Centinela Ave
Culver City, CA 90045

"Devoted Husband, Father & Grandfather. He seized life with joy. He gave to life generously. He leaves a legacy of love and laughter."

Don Adams (Maxwell Smart)

# 1923-2005

GET SMART

D on Adams died Sunday September 25, 2005, at Cedars-Sinai Medical Center from a form of lung infection. It was reported that he had broken his hip a year earlier and had been in poor health. He was 82. Two of his former wives and three of his children, as well as other family members, were with him when he died.

Donald James Yarmy was born April 13, 1923, in Manhattan. He grew up playing hooky from school and going to the movies. He joined the Marines at 16 by lying about his age. After the war he began stand-up comedy along with working at odd jobs. He changed his last name to his wife's maiden name because it started with an A. Often acting auditions were done in alphabetical order.

His break came after winning the Arthur Godfrey *Talent Scouts* competition in 1954, which led to his appearance on *The Steve Allen Show.* Adams most successful role was Adam Smart in *Get Smart* which he owned 33% of the show. It ran from 1965 to 1970. He won three Emmy Awards for the show. He also had a very successful voice-over career and appeared in commercials and other TV shows. Don was an avid gambler and an inveterate horseplayer. His leisure time was largely spent either at racetracks or in card games at the Playboy Mansion, and with pals such as Hugh Hefner, James Caan, and Don Rickles.

## Celebration of Life

A funeral Mass was held at the Church of the Good Shepherd in Beverly Hills. Those attending included long time friends Barbara Feldon, Don Rickles, Bill Dana and James Caan.

A memorial service was held a month later on October 5, 2005 at 7 p.m. at the Writers Guild Theater in Los Angeles.

## Final Resting Place

Hollywood Forever Cemetery
6000 Santa Monica Blvd
Los Angeles, CA  90038

**Don Adams**

April 13th 1923          Sept 25th 2005

Beloved husband, father and grandfather.
Proudly served his country during WWII
in the United States Marine Corps.

Comedian, poet, philosopher, movie buff
and never late for post time. A tough but
sensitive man with a sentimental heart
and a passionate soul.

He touched our hearts as Maxwell Smart,
secret agent 86 in the 1960's classic TV
series, "Get Smart" and filled the
world with laughter that will
forever be remembered.

*"Would you Believe..."*

# Elvis Presley

## 1935-1977

Elvis Presley died at approximately 3:30 p.m. on August 16, 1977 after suffering a heart attack. He was found face down in his bathroom and rushed to Baptist Memorial Hospital in Memphis, TN, where doctors tried to resuscitate him. It was reported that Elvis had high blood pressure, liver damage, glaucoma and an enlarged colon and at the time of death his body was pumped full of prescription pills. In 1973, he had overdosed twice on barbiturates.

Elvis Aaron Presley was born on January 8, 1935 in Tupelo, Mississippi. Jesse Garon Presley, his identical twin brother, was delivered 35 minute before him, stillborn. Presley's first public performance was when he was 10 years dressed as a cowboy performing "Old Shep." For his 11th birthday he received a guitar and started guitar lessons. Elvis didn't make his mark in music until 1956 when he met his long time manger Colonel Tom Parker. Elvis at that time was performing on the Louisiana Hayride and on as many tours and performances as possible. He was at first so nervous that his legs would shake and his wide-cut pants emphasized his movements, it later became his style. It was in 1956 that Elvis recorded his first big hit in Nashville called *"Heartbreak Hotel"* at RCA recording studio. Mega hits followed. "Hound Dog," "Don't Be Cruel," "Love Me Tender," "Peace in the Valley," "Teddy Bear," "Jailhouse Rock" to name a few.

Elvis purchased Graceland in 1957 for $102,000.00. He and his parents lived there the remainder of their life times. Also a resident at Graceland was Elvis' grandmother, Minnie Mae Presley.

On March 24, 1958, Presley was drafted into the U.S. Army. He was sent to Germany where he tried to serve as a regular solider. However his popularity and fame along with his continued records keep him in the media. Between his induction and discharge, Presley had ten top 40 hits. Also during his tour in Germany his mother, Gladys, passed away. He received an honorable discharge in 1960 and continued his successful career. In the 60s he began starring in moves and out of the 27 movies, 15 were accompanied by soundtracks from his albums.

Elvis and his music certainly influenced America. Some say he permanently changed the face of American pop culture. He tried to have a positive message to young people and keep true to his roots. His love of gospel music seemed to heal his soul when he needed it the most. Sales estimated between 600 million to 1 billion.

## Celebration of Life

Presley's funeral was on Thursday, August 18, 1977, at Graceland. Thousands of people gathered outside of Graceland to view the open casket. Fans were allowed to step inside the vestibule for a glimpse of Elvis' body and then directed back down the hill. However only about 200 close friends and family attended the funeral. JD Sumner was given the responsibility of planning the music. One of the songs sung at the funeral was a song Elvis loved and requested to be sung at many of his shows, "When It's My Time." It was sung by Bill Baize of the Stamps Quartet and written by Phil Johnson.

# Final Resting Place

Approximately 80,000 people lined the processional route to Forest Hill Cemetery, where Presley was laid to rest in a crypt as the same cemetery as his mother. Following an attempt to steal the singer's body in August, the remains of both Presley and his mother were relocated to Graceland's Meditation Garden on the grounds at Graceland.

Bob Denver

1935-2005

**B**ob Denver died September 6, 2005, at Wake Forest University Baptist Hospital in North Carolina of complications from cancer treatment. He had also undergone a quadruple heart bypass earlier that year. He was 70.

Robert Osbourne Denver was born January 9, 1935 in Rochelle, New York, and raised in Brownwood, Texas. He graduated with a degree in political science at Loyola University in Los Angeles, California. While there he performed in college productions. After college he taught physical education, math and history at a Catholic school in Pacific Palisades, California and worked as a mailman. It was while he was teaching he auditioned for the role as Maynard Krebs in the TV series *The Many Loves of Dobie Gillis* which aired on CBS from 1959 to 1963. The bearded beatnik who liked to play the bongos and hang out in coffee houses became a popular role for Denver.

When the series ended that roll was cast away and he became a castaway on the show *Gillian's Island*. His buster-brown hair cut with a white sailor hat and loveable character became his signature. It wasn't considered a smash hit even when it was canceled by CBS in 1967, but it continues to rerun today.

After *Gilligan's Island,* Denver went on to star in other TV series, including *The Good Guys* and *Dusty's Trail,* as well as to make numerous appearances in films and TV shows.

Denver left the limelight early to assist his wife in the care of their son who had severe autism and needed full time care. Like many actors back in that era they were not paid residuals from reruns so with very little personal wealth they started The Denver Foundation in an effort to help families who needed support with special needs.

## Final Resting Place

Cremated and location of ashes unknown.

We are proud of you 'Little Buddy!"

## Robin Williams

## 1951-2014

R obin Williams was found dead on August 11, 2014 from suicide by hanging in his Tiburon, California home. He was 63. Robin was in the early stages of Parkinson's disease and struggled with battles of depression, anxiety and had not shared his disease publicly. His family released a statement: *"On behalf of Robin's family, we are asking for privacy during our time of profound grief. As he is remembered, it is our hope the focus will not be on Robin's death, but on the countless moments of joy and laughter he gave to millions."*

Robin McLaurin Williams was born July 21, 1951 in Chicago, Illinois. Robin was very shy as a child but naturally funny. It wasn't until he got involved with the high school drama department that he began to overcome his shyness. He studied theater for three years at the College of Marin in Kentfield, California. He then got a full scholarship to Julliard. His classmates were Christopher Reeve and William Hurt. Williams performed in nightclubs before his role in the TV series, *Mork & Mindy* that aired in 1978 and ran for four seasons. He made his big-screen début in *Popeye* in 1980. He continued to have a string of successful film roles including *The Birdcage* (1996) and *Good Will Hunting* (1997). Williams battled drugs and alcoholism during his career. In 2009 he had heart surgery but had a full recovery and continued his successful acting career. He was nominated for an Academy Award for *Good Morning Vietnam*, (1987) *Dead Poets Society* (1989), *Fisher King* (1991).

## Celebration of Life

Family and friends paid their last respects at a private funeral service at Monte's Chapel of the Hills in San Francisco, California

Hundreds gathered for a public memorial six weeks after his death at the Curran Theatre in San Francisco.   Billy Crystal began the "Celebration of Life" with a tearful tribute.   Others who spoke included Whoopi Goldberg, Bonnie Hunt and Bobcat Goldthwait. All three of Williams' kids also spoke about their father.  Others in attendance were Seth Green, Eddie Izzard, Penny Marshall, Lance Armstrong, Pam Dawber, Bette Midler, Joel McHale, Jeff Bridges, Josh Groban, Marlo Thomas, Danny De Vito and Rhea Perlman and Ben Stiller. Those who attended were given wristbands with an image of a hummingbird and the message *"Love the stillness of life."*

Billy Crystal, his friend, hosted a Tribute to Robin at the 2014 Emmy Awards.

## Final Resting Place

Robin was cremated just a day after his death and autopsy. His ashes were scattered in the San Francisco Bay near his home.

The Williams family asked well-wishers to send contributions to charities close to the actor's heart in lieu of flowers. Suggested organizations include St. Jude Children's Research Hospital, Challenged Athletes, USO, the Muhammad Ali Parkinson Center, the Christopher and Dana Reeve Foundation and Glide Memorial Church in San Francisco.

Don Knotts died Friday night, February 24, 2006 of pulmonary respiratory complications (lung cancer) at Cedars-Sinai Medical Center in Beverly Hills. He was 81. Family members said that his longtime friend Griffith was one of his last visitors that night. He has been undergoing treatment in the months before his death.

Jesse Donald Knotts was born on July 21, 1924 in Morgantown, West Virginia. As a young man he started the world of entertainment as a ventriloquist. He attended West Virginia University prior to joining the Army during World War II and serving as an entertainer, then returned back to college to get his degree.

He got his big break in 1950 when me performed on *The Steve Allen Show.* His skit as a weatherman got him immediate attention.

He played the skinny, lovable nerd who kept generations of television audiences laughing as bumbling Deputy Barney Fife on *The Andy Griffith Show.*

He was allowed to carry one bullet in his shirt pocket after shooting himself in the foot. Although his career included seven TV series, it was the *Andy Griffith Show* that brought him TV immortality. The show ran from 1960-1968. The 249 episodes are still appearing in reruns.

In 1986 the actors reprised their roles for a television movie *Return to Mayberry* and in the 1970's he joined the case of the hit sitcom "Three's Company." He stayed on the show until it's final season in 1984.

His big screen success included *The Ghost and Mr. Chicken*, *The Incredible Mr. Limpet*, *The Reluctant Astronaut*, *The Shakiest Gun in the West*, *How to Frame a Figg*. And in 2005 Don provided the voice of "Mayor Turkey Lurkey" in Disney's animated film *Chicken Little*. It turned out to be his final films.

He received a star on the Hollywood Walk of Fame on January 19, 2000.

## Celebration of Life

Funeral services were held at 1:00 p.m. on Monday March 6, 2006 at Chapel of the Psalms in Lost Angeles with a reception following. His program read:

*Say not in grief "he is no more," but live in thankfulness that he was.*

## Final Resting Place

Westwood Memorial Park
1218 Glendon Ave,
Los Angeles, CA 90024

DON KNOTTS
1924 ~ 2006
HE SAW THE POIGNANCY IN PEOPLE'S PRIDE AND PAIN
AND TURNED IT INTO SOMETHING HILARIOUS AND ENDEARING

Glen Campbell

1936-2017

Glen Campbell died on Tuesday, August 8, 2017 from Alzheimer's disease, which he had been battling since 2011. He was 81.

Glen Travis Campbell was born April 22, 1936, in rural Billstown, Arkansas. He was one of 12 children and began playing a five-dollar guitar bought from a Sears Roebuck mail order catalogue, when he was four years old. After dropping out of high school at 16, he went out west with his uncle, living in Albuquerque as a bandleader and fill-in sideman. But it wasn't long before he made his way to Los Angeles, California where he got a job writing and recording demos.

His guitar and singing talents lead him to the his most famous studio contribution on the song, "I Get Around" by the Beach Boys. He continued to play on sessions, with an astounding 586 sessions in 1963 alone. His first recording as a featured singer was. "Gentle on My Mind." Then came his hits "The Time I Get to Phoenix," "Wichita Lineman," "Galveston," and "Rhinestone Cowboy." All of his No.1 hits on the country charts crossed over with success in the pop music world.

He had his own TV show, the *Glen Campbell Goodtime Hour,* between 1969-1972. His show was aired internationally giving him worldwide popularity. He released more than 70 albums and received nine Grammy Awards. He also moved into the film world as the co-star of John Wayne in the 1969 film *True Grit.* His song for the soundtrack was nominated for an Academy Award and Campbell was also nominated for Most Promising Newcomer at the Golden Globes.

Among his list of awards he was inducted into 2005 – Country Music Hall Of Fame in 2005 and Musician's Hall Of Fame in 2007.

Campbell once said he didn't consider himself a country singer, but a country boy who sings.

## *Celebration of Life*

Only one day after his death there was a private funeral and memorial held in Delight, AR. Glen's nickname to friends was Harry with his image adores every sign headed into the town of Delight.

There was a Memorial Service held on August 25, 2007 in Nashville to pay tribute to Glen Campbell by his fellow performers. It was held at the CMA Theater in the Country Music Hall of Fame. Dolly Parton was among many stars who paid tribute, describing Campbell as "one of the greatest voices of all time."

# *Final Resting Place*

Campbell was laid to rest in his hometown of 300 residents,
Delight Cemetery
Delight, AR 71940

# Special Notes of Interest

In 1976 **Burt Lancaster** said he had undergone so much plastic surgery over the years that his eyes were his only real facial feature. He wore a hairpiece in later films.

**John Ritter** died on his daughter's 5th birthday.

**Bud Abbott** split earnings 40/60 with partner, Lou Costello. He said comics were a dime a dozen. Good straight men were hard to find.

**Janet Leigh** was not nude in her shower scene in the Hitchcock movie *Psycho,* she wore a flesh-colored moleskin.

On the TV series *Bonanza*, **Michael Landon** who played "Little Joe" was the only cast member that did not wear a hairpiece.

**Hugh Hefner** pre-purchased the crypt space beside Marilyn Monroe for $75,000 in 1992 and has been laid to rest beside her. The crypt above Marilyn held a gentlemen who asked to be placed upside down facing her. After 23 years his wife sold the crypt for a reported 4.6 million and moved his body.

During **Roy Orbison**'s 1963 tour with the Beatles, Orbison left his glasses on the plane before a show. It forced him to wear his black frame, dark lense sunglasses for that night's show. Although he was embarrassed during the performance, the look became an instant trademark.

**Ricky Nelson**'s funeral service was held at the same chapel he had filmed a TV segment titled *Ricky Gets Married.*

**Elizabeth Taylor** converted to Judaism in 1959. She also hated being called Liz.

**John Wayne** was fluent in Spanish and Wayne's hair began to thin in the 1940s and he later began to wear a hairpiece.

**Michael Jackson** was a huge fan of *The Three Stooges* and even had a customized "Stooge" RV he drove around Neverland.

The tie-twiddle that **Oliver Hardy** did with his tie was used to convey a sense of coyness or embarrassment.

*My husband, **Phil Johnson**, wrote the song, "When It's My Time" which was sung at Elvis' funeral.

# Cemetery Section

# Visiting Cemeteries

Please be respectful at all times while visiting a cemetery. I would suggest not to go in groups and don't be loud. Remember while it is fun to find these awesome celebrities, others could be there burying their loves ones. Be considerate. If you see family members, do not disturb them. Give them the privacy they so richly deserve.

Also know the rules concerning private areas and photography. Although vandalism is rare, it has been reported from time to time. Don't be guilty of removing anything from the graves. John Wayne's gravesite didn't have a marker for years due to the fear of vandalism.

Use good sense and common courtesy while visiting. Don't try and clean the markers or headstones, other than removing leaves or mowed grass. The most thoughtful gesture could cause damage. Check with the office if you have questions about a gravesite condition.

Pay attention where you are WALKING. Don't walk directly across a grave if possible. Always walk around or between.

# Calvary Cemetery
4201 Whittier Blvd
Los Angeles, CA 90023

Calvary Cemetery is a Roman Catholic cemetery and spread out over one hundred and thirty-six acres and among the oldest cemetery in Los Angeles. Among it's many features are the *Stations of the Cross*. The outdoor natural stone Stations are placed at intervals along the main drive. People pray at the Stations every Sunday in Lent and in the month of November. The Calvary mausoleum has beautiful stained glass and hand-painted ceilings and is unique among local cemeteries in offering daily Mass- at 8:30 a.m. everyday except Sundays and holy days of obligation.

## Forest Lawn Memorial Park Glendale
1712 S. Glendale Ave.
Glendale, CA 91025

This 300-acre Cemetery is not your everyday cemetery. It is the resting place for over 150 million people. It is filled with towering trees, beautiful landscape lawns with splashing fountains and memorial architecture, an art gallery and is even a religious retreat for some. Pope John Paul II stopped here on one of his visited.

The art museum includes a respected stained glass collection and replicas of Michelangelo's statues with a swan-filled lake near by.

There are two mausoleums located at Glendale. The "Court of Honor" is publicly accessible and very patriotic. There are white steps that lead to the entrance with a large mosaic of the Declaration of Independence and a 13-foot statue of George Washington

The Great Mausoleum claims to have the world's largest religious painting, 195 feet in length by 45 feet high. This mausoleum is not as publicly accessible and there are no cameras allowed. To view the public areas you have to sign in and out. Michael Jackson's crypt is not accessible.

It has three non-denominational chapels: *"The Little Church of the Flowers"*, *"The Wee Kirk o' the Heather"* and *"The Church of the Recessional"*, which are all exact replicas of famous European churches. Over 60,000 people have actually been married here, including Ronald Reagan and Jane Wyman in 1940.

Unlike some of the other cemeteries, this cemetery was designed to captivate visitors but it also restricts and seems to discourage sightseeing by fans. Stars located here include: Humphrey Bogart, Nat King Cole, Walt Disney, Elizabeth Taylor, George and Gracie Burns, Red Skelton, The Lone Ranger, James Arness, Alan Ladd, Errol Lynn, Ted Knight, Jimmy Stewart, Spencer Tracy, Robert Young, Jean Harlow, and more.

# Forest Lawn Hollywood Hills
## 6300 Forest Lawn Drive
## Los Angeles, CA 90068

The creator of both Forest Lawn cemeteries, Hollywood Hills and Glendale, envisioned something more then a graveyard. He felt cemeteries should be more than bleak and depict, a beginning rather that and ending. When "The Builder" decided to open a second Forest Lawn location in the Hollywood Hills area, the local residents began to protest. So "The Builder" sent his staff to the county morgue and got 6 "John Does." During the night he had each one buried at the corners of the property. The next morning the protesters had no power because, by law, the property was now a cemetery. It opened in 1952.

Hollywood Hills is huge and feels a little patriotic with statues of George Washington and Thomas Jefferson and mosaic glass scenes depicting The Birth of Liberty. There are lush green rolling hills with manicured lawns. It overlooks Disney Studios, Universal Studios, and Warner Brothers and only 10 minutes west of the larger Forest Lawn cemetery in Glendale. Finding celebrity gravesites is rarely easy at any cemetery, and because Forest Lawn is so large and because no one on the grounds will assist you, it can be especially difficult here. However, it is well worth the hunt. I would suggest you start at the Court of Remembrance, which is a collection of outdoor mausoleum walls. There are some big names there (Carrie Fisher and Debbie Reynolds, Liberace, McLean Stevens, Sandra Dee, Forrest Tucker, Morey Amsterdam, Isabel Sanford, Freddie Prinze, Andy Gibb, Lou Rawls, Bette Davis and the original resting place of Lucille Ball.

*Note of Interest: Michael Jackson had his funereal here but was laid to rest at Forest Lawn Glendale located in The Great Mausoleum.*

# Hillside Memorial Park
## 6001 W. Centinela Ave.
## Culver City, CA 90045

Hillside Memorial Park is a Jewish cemetery and known for Al Jolson's towering 75-foot-high stone monument with a waterfall cascade. It is the most spectacular tomb in all of Hollywood and can be seen from the San Diego Freeway and it's only a few minutes from MGM studios.

Behind the Al Jolson monument is a large, two-story mausoleum with couches and lamps to create a home-like feel. The gold & white overhead lamps are shaped like Stars of David. The floors are tile with marble walls with fountains, glass doors, and sunny patio area lined with crypts. Almost all of the stars' tombs are located in this main white building which can be entered from the patio doors.

Some of the stars located here are: Shelly Winters, Neil Carter, Tom Poston, Susanne Pleshette, Gene Barry, Leonard Nimoy, David Janssen, and Jeff Chandler.

# Hollywood Forever
## 6000 Santa Monica Blvd
## Los Angeles, CA 90038

Hollywood Forever is a large picturesque cemetery that dates back to 1899 and includes some unusual shaped headstones , towering monuments and statues unlike you would see in a modern day cemetery. The history of this cemetery is engulfed with lawsuits and Ponzi-like schemes from previous owners. However it remains today restored and a wonderful place to visit.

This cemetery has been the backdrop location for a few Hollywood Movies including "Hot Shots" with Charlie Sheen , "L.A. Story" with Steve Martin and the TV show "Dexter." You can see the Hollywood sign through the north gates and south you can see the back lot of the Paramount Studios.

There are two indoor mausoleums, Abbey of the Psalms and Cathedral Mausoleum. Inside the Abbey of the Psalms the names of the various hallways and corridors are written on the tile floor. This helps with directions and finding your way around.

Just inside the Cathedral Mausoleum are large, white statues of the Twelve Apostles and St. Paul. Divided on each side of the hallway and at the corridors. Outside the Mausoleum you will find Toto from The Wizard of Oz on a pedestal. It reads, "There's No Place Like Home."

Right next to the Mausoleum is a beautiful marble tomb where Douglas Fairbanks Sr. and Jr. are buried that includes a water feature.

There is a new pavilion on the west side of the park with a private wing where July Garland's crypt is located.

Others located in this cemetery are Garland's childhood co-star Mickey Rooney, Rudolph Valentino, David White, Tyron Power, Darrin McGaven, Janet Gaynor, Jayne Mansfield and more.

*Special Note: When former Beatle, George Harrison passed away at a friend's house (Paul McCartney), his family had his body cremated by Hollywood Forever. His ashes were returned to the family and scattered in the sacred Ganges River in India.*

# Holy Cross Cemetery
### 5835 W Slauson Ave
### Culver City, CA 90230

Holy Cross is a very large Roman Catholic cemetery with over 200-acres of green sloping hillsides, and small ponds. The landscape is perfectly manicured with several grottos and waterfalls.

There are statues of St. Bernadette and the Virgin Mary that are great to use for directions to the volcanic-stone archway where many of the stars are located. This cemetery has round metal markers in the grass that allows you to easily pinpoint most graves.

There is a large white building at the top of a hill, which is the main mausoleum. Mausoleum entombment is an ancient Catholic tradition, yet also an ideal modern method of laying the dead to rest. As you enter the mausoleum it is very unexpected.

Inside is a small Catholic chapel (sanctuary) with an abstract painting of the Resurrection above the alter. The Chapel is absolutely beautiful with stain glass and clean lines. The walls are lined with crypts. It's amazing sitting in the pews looking toward the alter with wall lined names of those interred. There are openings on both sides that lead you down different hallways to view more crypts.

Some of the stars located here are: Rita Hayworth, Bing Crosby, Lawrence Welk, Sharon Tate and more.

# Inglewood Park Cemetery

720 E. Florence Ave
Inglewood, CA 90301

Inglewood Park Cemetery is over 100 years old but remains lovely with old-fashioned monuments, statues and a beautiful lake. It is only a few blocks from the Hollywood Park racetrack. The cemetery's predominantly African-America, but back in the day, this lush 340 acre park was where some of the stars were buried.

Inside the corridors of the Mausoleum of the Golden West you will find Betty Gable, Cesar Romero and Ray Charles. Others include, Ella Fitzgerald, Etta James. Jewel Akens, and Edgar Bergen among others.

There are beautiful venues for services including Grace Chapel among gardens, lakes and impressive statuary. Inglewood in unlike most cemeteries, it is a full service cemetery, mortuary, cremation and floral facility.

*Note of Interest: Both attorneys from the O.J. Simpson trial are buried here: Robert Kardashian and Johnnie Cochran.*

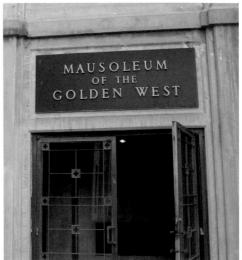

# Graceland Meditation Garden
### 3764 Elvis Presley Blvd
### Memphis, TN 38116

Meditation Garden was built by Elvis Presley in the mid sixties as a place for quite meditation next to his house. The Garden's center- piece is a circular twelve-foot fountain with five single jets of water and a large one in the middle all lit by colored floodlights. The curved wall behind the fountain is made of Mexican brick with four stained –glass windows. There is a large white marble monument of Jesus with outstretched arms and adorned with angel and cherubs inscribed "Presley" from his mother's original gravesite. It was dismantled and moved from Forest Hill Cemetery to Graceland when Elvis' body was relocated to Graceland.

Elvis, his mother, father, grandmother and a memorial plaque of his twin brother are all located there.

Graceland opens it's gates to Mediation Garden everyday from 7:30-8:30 a.m. where you can visit the graves at no charge. You must be off the premises at 8:30 to allow for paid tours that start at 9:00 am.

# Memorial Park Cemetery
5668 Poplar Avenue
Memphis, TN 38119

Memorial Park was established in 1925 against a backdrop of naturally rolling terrain with lakes, fountains, broad driveways, spacious lawns , beautiful trees and flowers.  The features include the Crystal Shrine Grotto-described as the only man-made crystal cave in the world. It also includes a Wishing Chair and Rose Garden, the Wishing Well, and Fountain of Youth.

# Mount Sinai Memorial Park
5950 Forest Lawn Drive
Hollywood Hills, CA 90068

Mt. Sinai Memorial Park is a Jewish cemetery that was acquired by Sinai Temple, the oldest and largest synagogue in Los Angeles in 1967.

There are different sections and one that includes a "Memorial to the Six Million," remembering the victims of the Holocaust. It also has a 150-foot-long mosaic mural depicting the history of the Jews in America. The park also features sculptures, fountains and carvings. Mt. Sinai is a more private cemetery by not publicizing any famous who are buried there. According to Jewish tradition there are no marker placed until one year after interment.

Some of the famous located here are Phil Silvers, Norman Fell, Marvin Hamlisch, Cass Elliott, Bonnie Franklin, Ross Martin and Don Rickles and more.

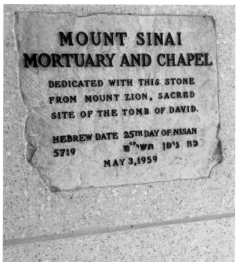

# Pacific View Memorial Park and Mortuary
### 3500 Pacific View Drive
### Corona Del Mar, CA 92625

One of the biggest stars of Hollywood is buried here instead of Hollywood, John Wayne. The 48 acre cemetery is located 15 miles south of Disneyland in the Newport Beach area in the heart of Orange county. You can view the California's shoreline from it's location. The residents admired Wayne so much they named a nearby airport after him. The John Wayne Airport is about four miles away.

Because the family feared grave robbers, they chose to leave his grave unmarked for almost 20 years. It now has a bronze plaque with an image of him on his horse near the Alamo. The beautiful green lawns has brooks and fountains.

*Reads:*

*"Tomorrow is the most important thing in life.*

*Comes into us at midnight very clean.*

*It's perfect when it arrives and it puts itself in our hands.*

*I hopes we've learned something from yesterday."*

# San Fernando Mission Cemetery
## 11160 Stranwood Ave
## Mission Hills, Ca  91345

This Catholic cemetery is near the San Fernando Mission and was founded in 1952 under a lease agreement from the Los Angeles Archdiocese. San Fernando Mission Cemetery is an active cemetery providing burials, entombments and cremation options to members of the Roman Catholic Community and their families.  It's a beautiful cemetery, but It's location is not close to any of the other cemetery's of the stars.  Bob Hope is one of the beloved performers located here. Others include Chuck Connors, Ed Begley, George Gobel, William Frawley and Walter Brennan.  In 2005 Bob Hope's remains were move to a special fenced location next to the Mission's Main Chapel.  There is a special garden that has a bowl like cover (which resembles the Hollywood Bowl) with the granite crypts of him and his wife in the middle.  There is a statue of "Our Lady of Hope" and a wall featuring a bronze photo of Bob Hope. The San Fernando Mission charges a small admission fee which now includes Hope's garden.

# Valhalla Memorial Park
### 10621 Victory Blvd
### Los Angeles, CA  91606

Pierce Brothers Valhalla Memorial Park has beautiful fountains, sculptures and archways.  There are religious statues throughout the landscaped sections. The cemetery is best known for its national architectural state called "Portal of the Folded Wings", honoring  the pioneers of the aviation industry.  There is a memorial to Amelia Earhart and others.  This cemetery is located south of the historic Burbank-Glendale Airport.

According to articles in the Los Angeles Times, this cemetery was involved in quit a few lawsuits during the 20s and 30s.  The state ended up with the ownership of the cemetery in the 1950s.  In 1991 final ownership was acquired by a new owner and is now part of the Dignity Memorial network.

In 2007 a 21-foot-long model of the Space Shuttle (the real shuttle is 122 feet long) was added.  In keeping with the theme of rebirth, the Space Shuttle memorial is also an example of creative recycling. It is, in fact, a former Hollywood movie prop, used in the ridiculous 2003 sci-fi disaster film *The Core*, where it played the Space Shuttle Endeavour.

# Woodall Cemetery
## Hwy 12
## Clarksville, TN 37043

Woodall Cemetery is a very small privately owned cemetery. It is located behind Mt. Hermon Baptist Church on Highway 12. The gates are left open for friends and family buried there. The Church is not affiliated with the cemetery nor does it keep records of who is buried there. However, funeral services are held at the church. The cemetery is old and very authentic. It is the resting place for the Tillis family.

# Pierce Bros Westwood Village Memorial Park
## 1218 Glendon Ave
## Los Angeles, CA 90024

This 2-½ acre cemetery is referred to by many as the, "hidden cemetery." The reason is because you could easily drive right past it among business and high-rise buildings. It is located on the south side of Wilshire Boulevard in Westwood. You cannot enter from the north, south or east sides- the only entrance is on the west side from Glendon Ave. However, it is a wonderful find! It is a smaller cemetery but has bigger than life stars resting there. The Chapel is small but has been the place for many celebrity funerals and memorials. There is a circular road that allows you to park and easily walk the grounds and find who ever you are looking for. Outdoor crypts line the walls and there is a beautiful memorial cremation garden.

Known as "the cemetery of tragic females" because so many buried there died young. The most famous females, being Marilyn Monroe. There is a memorial service held year on Aug 5, the anniversary of her death. There are also several unmarked graves including: Roy Orbison, Frank Zappa, and George C Scott.

Other celebrities you will find there are Richard Dawson, Rodney Dangerfield, Eddie Albert, Eve Arden, Fanny Brice, Sebastian Cabot, James Colburn, Bob Crane, ZaZa Gabor, Florence Henderson, Peggy Lee, Elizabeth Montgomery, Carl Wilson and more.

# Stars Cause of Death

Alan Hale Jr – Unknown Cancer

Andy Gibb – Myocarditis

Andy Griffith – Heart Attack

Andy Kaufman – Lung Cancer

Andy Warhol – Complications from Surgery

Anna Nicole Smith – Drug Overdose

Annette Funicello – Multiple Sclerosis

Anthony Perkins – Aids

Anthony Quinn – Pneumonia

Audra Lindley – Luekemia

Audrey Lindley – Appendiceal Cancer

Audrey Hepburn – Appendiceal Cancer

Ava Gardner – Pneumonia

Barbara Billingsley – Autoimmune
                          Disease

Barry White – Renal Failure

Bea Arthur – Unknown Cancer

Bea Benaderet – Lung Cancer

Bing Crosby – Heart Attack

Bob Hoskins – Pneumonia

Brittany Murphy – Pneumonia, Anemia,
                          Drug Intoxication

Buddy Ebsen – Pneumonia & Respiratory
                          Failure

Buddy Holly – Plan Crash

David Cassidy – Organ failure

Charlton Heston – Alzheimer's/ pneumonia

Dennis Weaver – Cancer

Don Rickles – Kidney failure

Donna Douglas – Pancreatic Cancer

Elizabeth Montgomery – Colorectal Cancer

Ernest Borgnine – Renal Failure

Errol Flynn – Heart Attack and Cirrhosis
                          of the Liver

Estelle Getty – Dementia

Ethel Merman – Brain Cancer

Etta James – Alzheimer's

Eva Gabor – Respiratory Failure

Fess Parker – Natural Causes

Gregory Peck – Pneumonia

Glenn Ford – Strokes

Harvey Korman – Aortic aneurysm

Jane Russell – Respiratory Failure

James Coburn – Heart Attack

Janis Joplin – Drug Overdose

Jane Mansfield – Car Accident

Jean Harlow – Renal Failure

Jean Stapleton – Natural Causes

Jessica Tandy – Ovarian Cancer

Jerry Lewis – Heart Disease

Jerry Orbach – Prostate Cancer

Jim Croce – Plane Cancer

Jim Varney – Lung Cancer

Joan Crawford – Pancreatic Cancer &
                          Heart Attack

Joan Rivers – Brain Damage during surgery

John Belushi – Drug Overdose

John Candy – Heart Attack

John Lennon – Murder Victim

Johnny Horton – Car Accident

Jonathan Brandis – Suicide by Hanging

Jonathan Winters – Natural Causes

Julia Child – Renal Failure

Karen Carpenter – Heart Failure &
                          Anorexia

Katherine Hepburn – Natural Causes

Larry Hagman – Throat Cancer

Larry Linville – Lung Cancer

Lauren Bacall – Stroke

Lee Marvin – Heart Attack

Lena Horn – Heart Failure

Leonard Nimoy – COPD

Leslie Gore – Lung Cancer

Leslie Nelson – Pneumonia

Lloyd Bridges – Natural Causes

Loretta Young – Ovarian Cancer

Louis Armstrong – Heart Attack

Lucille Ball – Abdominal Aortic Disease

Luther Vandross – Heart Attack

Janis Joplin – Drug Overdose

Jane Mansfield – Car Accident

Jean Harlow – Renal Failure

Jean Stapleton – Natural Causes

Jerry Orbach – Prostate Cancer

Mary Tyler Moore – Multiple ailments

Mike Conners – Leukemia

Patrick Swayze – Pancreatic Cancer

Paul Newman – Lung Cancer

Peter Graves – Heart Attack

Richard Montalban – Heart Failure

Richard Burton – Cerebral Hemorrhage

Richard Pryor – Heart Attack

Rita Hayworth – Alzheimer's disease

Robert Mitchum – Lung Cancer

Robert Prosky – Complications from
Surgery

Robert Reed – Colon Cancer

Robert Stack – Heart Attack

Robert Urich – Synovial Cell Sarcoma

Robin Gibb – Liver Cancer and Pneumonia

Rock Hudson – Aids

Rod Sterling – Complications from Surgery/
Heart Attack

Rodney Dangerfield – Complications from
Surgery

Roger Moore – Liver and Lung Caner

Ron Silver – Esophageal Cancer

Roy Rodgers – Heart Failure

Roy Schneider – Multiple Myeloma

Rudolph Valentino – Pleurisy & Brain
Inflammation

Russell Johnson – Renal Failure

Sammy Davis Jr. – Throat Cancer

Sandra Dee – Kidney Failure

Shari Lewis – Uterine Cancer

Sharon Tate – Murder Victim

Shelly Winters – Heart Failure

Shirley Temple – Lung Cancer

Slim Whitman – Heart Failure

Steve McQueen – Heart Attack

Susan Hayward – Brain Cancer

Suzanne Pleshette – Respiratory Failure

Telly Savalas – Bladder Cancer

Tom Bosley – Lung Cancer

Tony Curtis – Cardiac Arrest

Tony Randall – Pneumonia

Troy Donahue – Heart Attack

Vivian Vance – Breast Cancer

W.C. Fields – Stomach Hemorrhage

Wayne Rogers – Pneumonia

William Boyd – Heart Failure

William Conrad – Heart Failure

William Frawley – Heart Attack

Robert Crain – Murdered

Zsa Zsa Gabor – Heart Attack

# Man Wanted to be Buried with all His Money

"There was a man who had worked all of his life and has saved all of his money. He was a real cheapskate when it came to his money. He loved money more than just about anything, and just before he died, he said to his wife, 'Now listen, when I die I want you to take all my money and place it in the casket with me. Because I want to take all my money to the after life.'"

So he got his wife to promise him with all her heart that when he died she would put all the money in the casket with him.

Just as she promised she had a very nice funeral when he died. He was stretched out in the casket with his nicest suite, the wife sitting there in black next to their best friend. When they finished the ceremony, just before the undertakers got ready to close the casket, the wife said, 'Wait a minute!'

She stood up with a shoebox in her hand and placed it in the casket. Then the undertakers locked the casket and rolled it away."

"Her friend said, 'I hope you weren't crazy enough to put all that money in there with that stingy old man.' She said, 'Yes, I promised. I'm a good Christian, I can't lie. I promised him that I was to put that money in that casket with him." 'You mean to tell me you put every cent of his money in the casket with him?'

'I sure did,' said the wife. 'I got it all together, put it into my account and I wrote him a check.'"